PRAISE FOR COACH ORGERON

"Coach O saved my career, made me what I am today, and gave me the opportunity to prove myself, and for that, I'm forever grateful."

—HEISMAN TROPHY WINNER JOE BURROW, FIRST PICK OF THE 2020 NFL DRAFT

"Ed Orgeron was the first guy I hired when I got to USC, and his departure from our program to become a head coach himself was the biggest loss I had when somebody left. I've never been around a better recruiter, but he brought so much more than that to the Trojans. He puts all of his heart and soul into everything he does. I'm not surprised he led his beloved LSU Tigers to a national title. I couldn't be happier for him or his family because I know just how hard he's worked to earn all that he's accomplished."

—SUPER BOWL-WINNING COACH PETE CARROLL

"I've often said of Louisianans, they aren't *from* there, they are *of* there. It's as if they grew from the soil. Who else could connect with the state the way a man from Lafourche Parrish does? I felt that way *before* their season for the ages. Now, he could run for King. That team preached 'one heartbeat,' much like Ed's heart beats for the LSU Tigers. Always has. I believe he's the most perfect marriage of coach and program in all of sports."

—ESPN's SCOTT VAN PELT

FLIP THE SCRIPT

FLIP THE SCRIPT

LESSONS LEARNED ON THE ROAD TO A CHAMPIONSHIP

ED ORGERON
WITH BRUCE FELDMAN

NELSON BOOKS

An Imprint of Thomas Nelson

One Street Books

Flip the Script

Published in Nashville, Tennessee, by Nelson Books, an imprint of Thomas Nelson. Nelson Books and Thomas Nelson are registered trademarks of HarperCollins Christian Publishing, Inc.

Published in association with One Street Books and editor Lavaille Lavette.

Thomas Nelson titles may be purchased in bulk for educational, business, fundraising, or sales promotional use. For information, please e-mail SpecialMarkets@ThomasNelson.com.

Any internet addresses, phone numbers, or company or product information printed in this book are offered as a resource and are not intended in any way to be or to imply an endorsement by Thomas Nelson, nor does Thomas Nelson vouch for the existence, content, or services of these sites, phone numbers, companies, or products beyond the life of this book.

ISBN 978-1-4002-2518-7 (HC)
ISBN 978-1-4002-2520-0 (eBook)

Library of Congress Control Number: 2020942667

Printed in the United States of America
20 21 22 23 24 LSC 10 9 8 7 6 5 4 3 2 1

I am grateful for my dad and mom, Bebe and Coco, who dedicated their whole life preparing me to be the man I am today. I grew up rich in their home because they gave me courage, toughness, the ability to compete, and the ability to communicate—and for their unconditional love, support, and understanding. For that, I am forever grateful to them.

I would also like to dedicate this book to my three sons—Parker, Cody, and Tyler. They are the most valued parts of my life. I know that they will pass on the same Orgeron traits to their kids that my parents passed on to me.

Geaux Tigers.

CONTENTS

CONTENTS

FOREWORD

by Dwayne Johnson

Coach O is a winner. A national champion. He's a winner in the game of football and the game of life. But he's only a winner because he knows what it's like to lose.

Ed Orgeron knows what it's like to hit rock bottom and instead of staying there, he pulled himself up, became accountable, and eventually went on to become one of the most influential and successful coaches in college football history. I had the privilege of being coached by him while playing with arguably the most dominant defensive line college football has ever seen at the University of Miami.

I learned many tough, intense and smart lessons from Coach O. Lessons that would go on to influence my career and how I conduct my business today. And that will always be the mark of a GREAT FOOTBALL COACH—when he teaches a player how to win beyond the gridiron.

Congrats, Coach O, on your book, *Flip the Script: Lessons Learned on the Road to a Championship.* Cheers to the lessons and cheers to the journey.

—Dwayne Johnson

INTRODUCTION

I wrote this book to share my story about what happens when you become totally honest with yourself and come to terms with your own strengths and weaknesses—much like a coach would when assessing any recruit or opponent. Total honesty doesn't mean putting limits on yourself; rather, it enables you to set up environments where you—and everyone else around you—can thrive and grow.

I'll tell you how LSU evolved into a program that went 15–0 and beat more top-ten opponents than anyone in the history of college football. But that change is really a by-product of something that goes far beyond the lines of a football field. You'll see what can happen when you open yourself up to making drastic changes and—in the case of the LSU Tigers—create the culture and innovations that help put you and your team in a prime position every Saturday.

This is my step-by-step journey of running up the coaching ladder and then plummeting all the way back down as I came to terms with my battles with addiction and the lessons I learned from it. I share how I set a new standard and all that it took to flip the script for myself and for the team, as I learned from both my mistakes and the mistakes of others. More than anything, this book will explore what can happen when you believe in a bigger plan, refuse to let anyone else define you, and never give up.

◀1

GETTING FIRED

◀

My whole life, not just my coaching career, has reached the highest of highs. It has also hit the lowest of lows—as low as any coach has ever experienced. When we step back and see the mind-bending twists and turns—how so many were completely out of our control—we begin to grasp that something much bigger than ourselves is driving it all. But when we're grinding away in the middle of it, we're pretty oblivious to that.

The one thing I've always tried to do is learn from all my experiences—especially my mistakes. Those experiences shaped me as a person, a parent, and a leader. They've prepared me for where I am today and who I am today. And as a result I am able to handle more than I ever could before. These days, nothing—whether that be an issue with a player, a staff member, an opponent, or anything off the field—could come across my desk that would surprise me. And there's nothing I couldn't learn from. In fact, the low times have taught me the most—they've made it apparent that I had to do something different, to flip the script in my life, or in my coaching. That's a skill that anyone can use to turn a disaster into a win.

And I can tell you now, one of my biggest disasters turned out to be—in the long run—one of my biggest wins. What most people thought was pretty much the end of my career as a head coach actually turned out to be the beginning of it.

◀

For three years when I was the head coach at Ole Miss, we had a string of *almosts* and *what-ifs* against one top-ten team after another. In 2006, during my second year, we lost in overtime at Louisiana

3

State University when they were a 27-point favorite. Early in my third season, we had almost beaten number-three-ranked Florida and Tim Tebow, who were the defending national champs. It was frustrating to be so close and lose, but I kept thinking, *Man, we're almost there. We're almost there.* I was waiting for that breakout win. We were just a couple of plays away.

So when we played against Alabama in 2007, I had high hopes. This could be it for us. And honestly, this critical win could be what took my career out of the danger zone.

It was also the first time I ever coached against Nick Saban. It was Saban's first season at Alabama and my last one at Ole Miss. Coach Saban had already won one national title at LSU, and over the next decade he would win five more. He is considered by many to be the top coach in the history of college football. I'm sure a lot of people at that point would have seen me on the opposite end of the spectrum.

Alabama was 4–2 that season and we were 2–4. I still felt like we were really close to having that big turn-the-corner win for our program.

I knew we had recruited well. Most of our best players were freshmen and sophomores. Some had to play before they probably were ready, but they were the best we had. My first signing class had five guys who ended up playing in the NFL, including two first-round draft picks (Peria Jerry and Michael Oher), a future Pro Bowl wide receiver (Mike Wallace), and BenJarvus Green-Ellis, who had two thousand-yard rushing seasons. Our second recruiting class had eight guys who became NFL players. We ended up landing a really talented quarterback transfer from Texas, Jevan Snead, but he wouldn't be eligible till the next season, so we never had a chance to play him in a game.

We went toe-to-toe with Saban's team that afternoon in 2007. We had a 24–17 lead in the fourth quarter before a long punt return and Bama interception return gave them a 27–24 lead. We had the ball near midfield in the game's final minute and faced a fourth-and-twenty-two.

Our quarterback, Seth Adams, heaved the ball deep along the left sideline, and Shay Hodge leaped and snatched the ball out of the hands of a Tide defensive back to set us up at the Alabama four-yard line with seven seconds remaining. Our sideline erupted. The whole stadium was rocking.

We were going for the win. I was sending in our best player, Greg Hardy, a six-foot-five defensive end who also played for the Ole Miss basketball team. We were gonna flex him out away from the line of scrimmage in one-on-one coverage and throw him a jump ball on a fade pattern into the corner of the end zone. Hardy had been dominant all afternoon. He had thirteen tackles, five tackles for a loss, and three sacks that day. He'd caught a touchdown pass in our opener, and I was confident he was about to catch one in this game too.

And then Saban called a timeout. And the refs deliberated. And deliberated. The play happened on their sideline, and he'd gotten in the refs' ears. I thought, *There's no way they're going to overturn that—how could they overturn it?*

Saban argued that Shay Hodge had run out of bounds and reentered the field to make the catch, which would make him an ineligible receiver. But to overturn the call, the officials would have had to rule that not only had Shay run out of bounds—and done so on his own—but also that he was the first to touch the ball. It didn't appear from replays that either of those things could have been determined conclusively.

How did you not see him pushing me out of bounds? Even if they didn't see him force me out of bounds, I wasn't the first player to touch the ball. Their defensive back caught the ball a little before me. I was pulling it out over his hands.

—*SHAY HODGE, FORMER OLE MISS RECEIVER*

After five minutes, the refs overturned the call—and we lost the game. Not only that, but we lost that critical emotional boost it would have given us. That victory would have given the team confidence to go on to win other games. It might have turned that program around.

Instead, we had yet another *almost* on our hands. When that game ended, I thought, *Oh, here we go again.* And at that point, "close enough" didn't count. There were no moral victories in football.

A lot of folks came up to my family after the game and told them we'd been robbed. My wife, Kelly, had thought that because we were in the middle of the Bible Belt, many of those same people were going to think, *Well, maybe this just wasn't meant to be.*

As hard as that was to believe at that time, I think she saw it that way—that there was a bigger plan in place. When you're in the middle of it, you can't grasp that bigger-picture thinking. But, after really looking back at my journey, all the twists and turns extending far beyond my time at Ole Miss, it becomes obvious there was a bigger plan at play.

It turns out, part of that plan was for me to get to that school in Oxford, Mississippi, and make my mistakes, so I could learn enough to eventually get a job at the place I grew up dreaming about: LSU. All those adverse circumstances were giving me phenomenal training.

But at the time, we were all feeling the heavy atmosphere of a losing season—even my twin sons, Cody and Parker, who were nine at the time.

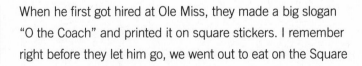

When he first got hired at Ole Miss, they made a big slogan "O the Coach" and printed it on square stickers. I remember right before they let him go, we went out to eat on the Square in Oxford and noticed that someone had made up stickers that said "O's Gotta Go" and stuck them all over, on stop signs and everywhere. We went around pulling down those stickers. That's when it really hit me that, man, my dad's in a cutthroat business.

—*CODY ORGERON*

A month after the Alabama game, we faced our archrival, Mississippi State, about a hundred miles away in Starkville. It's called the Egg Bowl, our biggest game of the year—and definitely the fiercest for the fans. Our athletic director, Pete Boone, and the school chancellor, Robert Khayat, had given me public votes of confidence in the previous month. Khayat had told the Associated Press my job was safe, but I didn't know what to believe. Reporters were coming up to me before the game saying they heard I was getting fired whether we beat Mississippi State or not.

I thought that if I won that game, they'd have to keep me.

Our guys played hard. We led 14–0 in the fourth quarter. We had fourth-and-one around midfield with about ten minutes left in the game. I told the staff on the headset, "Let's go for it." Usually, someone might counter and say, "I think we should punt," but nobody else said a word. I went for it because I wanted to crush them. It was a big rivalry game.

We called a running play and got stuffed. Two minutes later, they scored a touchdown, and then ran a long punt return back for another score. We dropped passes. I was thinking, *Oh, s****. I'd never in my life seen the tables turn like that. Everything went their way. We lost 17–14.

I knew it was over for me at Ole Miss.

Trying to leave that stadium was a nightmare. We had no police or security around to help us get our busses out of there. It seemed like there were thousands of rival Mississippi State fans by our busses ringing their cowbells. We sat for what seemed like half an hour. It was brutal. When I got home that night, I was in such pain that I had to go straight upstairs to sleep. I was so sick to my stomach that I'd made that call and lost the game.

The next morning, Pete Boone called me into his office. It was a very short meeting.

"Sorry, Ed. It was one of those days."

I knew he was firing me. I said, "Okay, good. Thank you."

I hadn't won enough games.

I called my wife and then called a meeting to tell the staff. Everybody had the chance to talk. I thanked the guys for all of their hard work and tried to give them some closure. I wanted to end things on a positive note. But we had a pretty tense time limit. The school told us we had two hours to get out of the building before the police would come to escort us away. My wife and I packed up all of my stuff and as we were leaving, the police showed up to make sure we were getting out of there.

◀

Despite our police escort, I was happy it was over. Our whole family had been miserable there for three years.

Every morning before I went into the office at Ole Miss, my wife and I would have coffee and talk. My second week on the job, just before I left for work, I told her, "We'd better save our money. They don't want me here." I just felt it. I knew the margin of error there was very small. We didn't have the resources that the other SEC schools had, both in finances and facilities. I could also just feel it inside my gut that the athletic director didn't want me there as the head coach.

The atmosphere was toxic. The media mocked me and made

fun of my voice and accent. They called me Coach Zero. One local talk radio host made up a song that had a "YAW YAW YAW" chorus, ridiculing how I spoke. It was pretty vicious. My youngest boys—our twins, Cody and Parker—had been seven when we got to Oxford. My oldest, Tyler, was thirteen. They had to hear constant criticism of me when they were at school. They never told me about it, but I know they had to deal with hearing their father getting ridiculed. So the day I got fired, it was a weight off our shoulders.

I was still eating breakfast with my brothers Parker and Tyler sitting at the kitchen counter. My mom got a call on our home line and we heard her say, "It happened?" I put two and two together. She hung up and went, "Well, boys, it happened." So we went to the IPF (Ole Miss's indoor practice facility where the coaching offices were) and were standing on the turf, expecting him to be all down. He came through the glass doors with this huge smile on his face—saying "Woo hoo!" We could tell he was genuinely excited to get out of there. He said, "Well boys, we get to leave Oxford!"

—CODY ORGERON

That night we all actually danced around in our living room together. We were getting out of there!

◀

The hardest part of getting fired was knowing that we were close. I know people didn't see it that way, but it was true. There was a lot of good happening—especially on the recruiting front. But I wish I wouldn't have had to go as hard on the players and assistants like I did.

We got out of Oxford and drove to Destin, Florida, for a few days of vacation. While the boys played on the beach, I did some soul searching. I don't know why, but I had the feeling I would get a chance to be a head coach again. I started taking notes, strategizing about how to improve, and studying the things I needed to do to be a better coach.

I called a friend. I was complaining about things—the Ole Miss administration, that I didn't have enough time, that we were just a year away, that there was dissension on the coaching staff, that I didn't have enough players when I got there. He listened for a while then said, "Whoa, whoa—wait a minute. The only person you can change is you. If you want to coach again, you're going to have to change the things you did wrong. Now, these things may have occurred at Ole Miss or they may not have, but if you don't make some changes with how *you* handle things, you're never going to change as a coach."

He made the point that I needed to change inside. I needed to change how I dealt with things.

That was critical for me to hear. I thought a lot about the Serenity Prayer that we often recite at our AA meetings: "God grant me the serenity to accept the things I cannot change, the courage to change the things I can, and the wisdom to know the difference." When it comes right down to it, the only people we can control are ourselves. So I had to look at why I hadn't had success.

Some of those things I had complained about were probably true, but first I needed to realize that I had to work on myself.

After taking his advice, I started listening and observing other coaches closely, listening to their interviews, what they said after the game, what they were doing, how they tried to run things. I think we did a lot of the right things at Ole Miss to get that program turned around. Maybe people began to realize that after Houston Nutt came in and went to back-to-back Cotton Bowl games with the players we'd recruited. At the same time, my record in my three years was what it was—10–25. When you're not winning, people tend to want to believe the worst, and that can create an echo chamber that can seep inside your program. You've got to learn to block out that noise and convince those around you to block it out too.

◀

The truth is, had I not been fired, or even if our season had gone a little better with a couple more wins, I wouldn't have been as open to making changes. I could have been stubborn and convinced myself, *Oh yeah, we were definitely on the right track and it was working just fine—we only needed more time.* But when you have the results we did, you need to be honest with yourself and be open to fixing what doesn't work.

When I was in it at Ole Miss, it was a fight every day. I knew my back was against the wall. I was determined to go as hard as I could because I was hearing they wanted to get rid of me. I never wanted to be 7–6. I didn't aspire to be 7–6 or 8–5. I always thought about bringing Ole Miss to a Sugar Bowl and playing in the Dome. Losing that coaching job was the first time I had ever gotten fired for my coaching. After all that struggle, it lit a fire under me, and I knew I had to change.

As I reflected there at the beach, as I studied and did my soul searching, I realized I had to treat coaches better than I had at Ole Miss. I was really hard on my coaches, yelling at them and cussing at them. I felt bad about it then, and I still feel bad about it now. I've apologized to many of them. But I wasn't going to make that mistake again.

I also realized that I needed to just be nicer to my players. I needed to be more like an uncle or father to them instead of a coach.

I realized I needed to be the guy who had connected with them when they were recruited.

Wherever I ended up next, they were going to get a new and improved Coach O. I just had to figure out where the old Coach O had come from first—and find a way to get back to my roots, back to the place where my love of football started.

◄2

| | | | | | | | | | |

BEBE

Way before I was "Coach O," I was Bebe (pronounced *bay-bay*)—the French word for *baby*. My dad was Bebe, too, because he was my grandparents' twelfth child—and supposed to be their last, although they ended up having another. He started working on the tugboats as a deck hand when he was fourteen and eventually worked himself up to being a superintendent at the local phone company. My mom is Coco. Her father was a trapper, and when she and her sister were growing up, from the time they were nine years old, they skinned muskrats to help out the family business. When she wasn't cooking for us and helping us with school, she worked at a furniture store. I was the oldest of their two sons.

We grew up in a remote corner of the bayou, about an hour southwest of New Orleans. My momma's family's roots there go back six generations. Our home was Lafourche Parish (pronounced La-*foosh*), and we lived in a tiny town of about seven thousand people called Larose. Everyone from down there still knows me as Bebe.

My brother, Steve, and I were raised in a house right on the bayou that my parents rented for twenty-five dollars a month. I knew from the time I was little how hard my parents worked to provide for us. We never owned a home, but I always had twenty dollars in my pocket. We never took a vacation as a family. Never went out to eat. But my dad always seemed to make time to coach me and the other kids in the neighborhood in our backyard football games.

I was always big for my age and pretty rough. By the time I was six, I was playing tackle football with the twelve-year-olds. Our field was a patch of grass surrounded by gravel driveways, littered with rocks and shells. A sewer ditch was our fifty-yard line. The bushes were our sidelines. It always got really competitive. I think every game ended with a fight. We played sports all the time—every sport. All my cousins lived in the neighborhood.

We all grew up loving LSU. Everybody loves LSU down there. Our area produced some great players for the school, so we all felt we had a special connection to the place. Ronnie Estay, Arthur Cantrelle, and Joe LaBruzzo were my idols when I was a little kid. We lived for those Tiger football games on Saturday nights, huddled around the radio, listening to the calls on WWL.

Just thinking about the LSU Tiger Marching Band playing the first few bars of "Hold That Tiger"—"Duh-DA-duh-DAH!"—still puts goose bumps on my arms. From the time I was six years old, I'd told my daddy I was going to be a coach. It's just something I always wanted to do. It's something I always believed that I was wired for, and that I'd be really good at. But I needed an education first.

◀

My mother and father never let me fish or hunt. They wanted me to get an education and get out of Larose. When I was about twelve, my mother pulled me aside and made me promise her that I would get an education. She said, "You gotta promise me, son! There's not a lot of hope without an education." About a week later, my father pulled me aside and said he wanted me to get an education, too, but admitted to me that he couldn't afford it—so he said, "You'd better get a scholarship."

I never wanted to disappoint my mother or let my father down. I understood where they were coming from. They didn't want me to have to grow up the hard way like they had.

Down there in the bayou, we started drinking early. I had my first beer at age ten. At twelve, I'd go to weddings at the VFW and sneak beers. By the time I was thirteen, I'd grown to about six foot one, 220 pounds. I didn't look my age. By fifteen, I was hanging out at the bars drinking. The people who worked there would usually say something like, "I know who you are. Be careful." And they were right—I had plenty on the line.

◄

I was serious about football. I loved the physical nature of the game, but also the tactical side of it. I loved how each individual battle on a play represented such a key role in whether the whole game was successful or failed. I also loved our high school coach at South Lafourche High—Ralph Pere. I idolized him. He had played offensive line at LSU in the sixties and was an all-conference player. And he was a stud. Like a second father to me. Coach Pere was tough as heck. He was about six foot three, 280 pounds, and everybody was scared of him. We knew he really cared about us—but you didn't want to cross him. He'd have us hitting that five-man sled for what sometimes seemed like half of practice. *Hit-and-drive! Hit-and-drive! Hit-and-drive!*

I made the varsity team as a sophomore and started both ways at tackle. Our team in 1977 was special. Our quarterback was my old friend Bobby Hebert, who was a senior and lived in Cut Off, Louisiana, a few miles from me in the next town over. Bobby used to tell everybody we were related, but I'm not sure if that's really true. He was a great player and a great leader. Joe Burrow actually reminded me a lot of Bobby. They were both so smart and poised. Both were really good basketball players, and you believed in them so much that no matter what, they were going to make the play when you needed it. Bobby, though, was definitely a lot more flamboyant than Joe. We used to call Bobby "Rubber Band" because he was so skinny. He was like a baby fawn. He just had to grow into his body.

We all played hard for Coach Pere and for each other. We knew we weren't the most talented team, but we had a close bond. One game that season, against one of our rivals, H. L. Bourgeois High School, my helmet had come down right above my eye and given me a nasty gash. At halftime, the trainer looked at it and told me he couldn't give me a numbing shot because it'd swell up so bad I wouldn't be able to see out of it. I said, "Screw it. Just stitch it up." There was blood all over the place. I still have the scar on my eyelid. That's how determined we all were to play our best.

We had to beat Archbishop Shaw High in the state quarterfinal playoff. They had a great quarterback in John Fourcade, who went on to play at Ole Miss and then for the Saints. If we played them a hundred times, I think they would have beaten us ninety-nine times. But we beat them in the one game that mattered, to advance to the title game.

◀

On the morning of the state championship game, I woke up and smelled fried shrimp. I thought I had to be dreaming. But then my mom kicked the door open. She had a shrimp po-boy in one hand and some blue-and-white pom poms in the other, and she had my football helmet on. On my way to the stadium, I remember thinking, *We'd better win this game or she'll kick my ass.*

We ended up winning the state title on a fourth-and-twenty-seven play. We were trailing 20–14. Bobby, our quarterback, walked into the huddle and said that we were going to make the play. He took the snap and tried to hit the dig route. The defensive back hit the ball into the air and our receiver caught it—and we scored the touchdown. Then, they partially blocked the extra point, but the ball still got over the goal post. We won, 21–20. It was something none of us will ever forget. To win like that with your brothers was priceless.

◀

After we won that championship, Alabama started recruiting me hard. One of their assistants told me he was going to bring Bear Bryant to my house, but LSU was recruiting me hard too. My daddy said, "Ain't no reason for Bryant to come to the house. You're going to LSU."

Before I left for Baton Rouge, I trained with my uncle Mike. He was the one who'd taught me how to lift weights. During the day he worked as a teacher, so we ran at nights around his schedule. When I got up to LSU, I was not ready for that heat in Baton Rouge—or their pace. I wasn't in shape. We had two weeks of freshman practice to catch up before the varsity came in.

That LSU freshman class was loaded. We had Albert Richardson, Ramsey Dardar, and Leonard Marshall, with Alan Risher as quarterback. I really struggled. Most of the guys were faster. I weighed about 240 pounds and ran a 5-flat 40. So they moved me over to the offensive side and put me at center, probably rightfully so, because I ran okay, but not like those D-linemen did. But I'd never played center before. I had never hit a one-man sled. I had trouble doing that. Plus, other things were weighing on me off the field.

I'd become friends with Ramsey and a few of the other guys, but I was still homesick. I'd never been away from home before. I had been there about three weeks. I didn't have a roommate. I felt like I couldn't handle being there, being just another guy, away from home.

On our first off day, a Sunday, I decided to get in my blue Grand Prix and head home. I didn't tell a soul where I was going or what I was doing. I made the two-hour drive home, the whole time thinking, *What am I doing?* I didn't think I was ready for college ball. I didn't think I was good enough. Deep down, I knew I was making a big mistake by quitting.

When I pulled into my parents' home in Larose, my daddy had that look on his face when he saw me that said, C'mon? Really? I knew they were concerned.

> I lost ten pounds when he was away at LSU. And if you know me, I don't lose ten pounds unless you drag me behind a car. Me and my son are close, close, close. I didn't want him to come home. Other people travel all the time. We stayed at home. Every day, every meal, I cooked from scratch. He wasn't worldly. We were sitting on the swing when he pulled up. He went in his room. There was just a sadness we all felt.
>
> —COCO ORGERON

The LSU coaches called my house the next day to talk to my dad. I heard my dad tell them, "I've never seen my son like this." He knew I didn't want to go back to LSU. He could read what was in my heart.

The next morning before dawn, my daddy woke me up and told me I was going to work with him digging ditches. He handed me a shovel and we jumped in his truck to go to his work site. We were alongside the road, so anyone could drive by and notice me, realizing that I'd quit LSU football to come home. I heard all sorts of stuff. One guy stopped and rolled down his window. "You couldn't take it. You're a quitter!"

I felt like I'd let everybody in the community down—especially my mom and dad. I'd never quit anything before. It was humiliating. It felt like I'd gone from the penthouse to the outhouse in one day.

◀

I stayed at my parents' home that entire fall, working with my dad and taking classes part-time at Nicholls State. In November, my old quarterback Bobby Hebert called me asking if I wanted to play with him at Northwestern State up in Natchitoches, Louisiana. I didn't even know where Natchitoches was, but I said, "Hell, yeah—I want to play."

> I told Bebe, "If you come up here, I know you're going to play right away. You can room with me." In Northwest Louisiana, you might as well be in Texas. It was a lot different than South Louisiana. We used that to our advantage with our accent. The girls treated us like we were some of those foreign tennis players! But when Bebe came up there, the only thing his daddy told me was, "Bobby J, you make sure he goes to class." I promised him that, so even though we were missing curfew a lot, no matter what condition we were in, we were making it to class.
>
> —*BOBBY HEBERT*

The coaches at Northwestern State trusted Bobby. He had told them about the kind of player I was. They knew if LSU had wanted me, I could make a big impact there. And I wanted to play again. When I got there, I was hungry. I got to stay on the defensive line and had a blast playing with a lot of my buddies. There was a lot of talent there. Bobby played in pro football for fourteen years and was the MVP of the United States Football League championship game. Our running back, the late Joe Delaney, was AFC Rookie of the Year for the Kansas City Chiefs. Mark Duper played in a bunch of Pro Bowls for the Miami Dolphins, and Gary Reasons won a couple of Super Bowls with the New York Giants. We had some great players. Great guys too.

In the summers, me and our nose tackle, Bryan Arceneaux, who grew up down the road from me, shoveled shrimp at the docks. Sometimes we worked eighteen-hour shifts for five dollars an hour, depending on how many boats pulled in with thousands of pounds of shrimp. They put you at the bottom of the boat with a shovel and told you to get to work. At twelve o'clock, they'd blow a horn and lower down a bucket with our lunch in it. I can still hear the *eek-eek-eek* sound of them cranking it down to us. We'd each get a lunch-meat sandwich with one piece of lunch meat on it, a bag of Lay's potato chips, and a Coke. We had twenty minutes to eat. Then they'd crank the bucket up—*eek, eek, eek*—and it was back to shoveling. Sometimes until eleven or twelve at night—and we'd be up the next morning to start by 6:00 a.m.

We slept near the docks in a twelve-by-twelve-foot cabin with no electricity or running water. The smell of the dead shrimp was so bad we almost wanted to quit for that reason alone. It was hard work, but we wanted to make some quick money, and in the end, we made good friends with all the people. At the end of the summer, we brought a lot of shrimp back to school to sell it at a higher price. We took all that money, bought beer, and got ready for the season.

◀

I'd made a shaky start at LSU, but at Northwestern State I was finding my footing. John Thompson, the defensive coordinator, was one of the first people to recognize that I had the makings of a coach—and one of the first to encourage me.

> I remember vividly the first meeting that I had with him. I was like twenty-six, making $18,000 a year and had come from Bible Belt Arkansas. I was still in penny loafers and button downs. That wasn't a penny loafers crowd. I'd heard Bebe was the leader, the bell cow. He came in wearing torn jeans and a T-shirt. There was nothing phony about him. That was my first introduction to Cajun culture. His attitude was, "I'm going to be the leader. We're going to get this done." I'd never seen anybody like that. The guys followed Bebe because of how hard he played and how hard he lived. He had such a fire, unlike any I'd ever seen, or even seen since then. Bill Johnson and I immediately wanted to hire him as a graduate assistant, thinking at the time that we'd never seen anybody who could get in the street with those players and then the next day command all of their respect, working the heck out of them, and they gave it all for him. He had something about him that could still be real, and people would respond to him. That blew me away.

> *—JOHN THOMPSON, FORMER NORTHWESTERN STATE*
> *DEFENSIVE COORDINATOR*

We had a lot of good times in Natchitoches. I started all four years at defensive end and was voted a captain my senior year in 1983. Looking back, if I'd have stayed at LSU, I think I could have been a really good center. I had to get bigger and stronger. By my redshirt sophomore year—my third season in the program—I think I would have been the starting center. But things worked out at Northwestern State.

◀

After I graduated, I had a one-day tryout with the Memphis Showboats of the USFL but didn't make it. I called my daddy right after. I stopped at a truck stop in Tennessee to use the payphone.

"You done?"

"Yeah."

"What are you gonna do?"

"I wanna be a football coach."

"Go get it."

I figured my best hope to break into coaching was at my alma mater. I asked Sam Goodwin, who I played for at Northwestern State, if he had any room on his coaching staff. He said, "I don't have a position for you."

I said, "I don't care. I'm going to start coaching for you." He said, "Bebe, you can be a student assistant, but you can't live in that dorm."

So, I took a cot and moved into the visitors' dressing room of the stadium, and I lived there for the whole season. I loved it. I'm grateful that Bill Johnson, my defensive line coach with the Demons, and John Thompson, the defensive coordinator, let me coach.

I coached our guys hard. The next year, I followed Bill Johnson to McNeese State and became a graduate assistant there. The following summer I was back shoveling shrimp and living in a small shack near the Gulf of Mexico.

One morning the phone rang on the deck.

"Bebe, you got a call from Arkansas."

It was Brad Scott on the line, who I knew from Northwestern State. He said, "There is an assistant strength coach job at the University of Arkansas. It doesn't pay much though. Do you want it?"

I said, "Hold on." I threw the shovel in the bayou and yelled into the receiver, "Hell, yeah! I am comin'. Now, where is Arkansas?"

He said it was about ten hours from there, and I said I'd be there the next morning.

I took a shower, changed, and drove off to Arkansas. I got to live in the dorm for free and got a twenty-five-dollar check every two weeks. Thank God my parents always gave me a hundred dollars a week to spend.

My boss was the head strength coach, George Williford. I'd clean the weight room every day and mop all the floors—and I was happy to do it. I was fired up to work there. I got to work every morning at 5:00 a.m. The football coaching staff offices looked out at the weight room, and they would always see how excited I was to be there. Head coach Ken Hatfield and defensive coordinator Fred Goldsmith were great to me.

On Thursday mornings, all the guys on the team who missed class would be given extra workouts as a penalty—I'd be the one to work them out. I drove one of them in particular extra hard. It turns out a lot of people treated this guy with kid gloves. Another one of the assistant strength coaches had seen me working the guy out and said, "Man, you are one crazy son of a gun. You do know who that is, right?"

I said, "Yeah, that's Stephen. He plays outside linebacker for us. He's number 15."

He said, "Well, that's Jerry Jones's son. You know who that is, don't you?"

I said, "Man, I'm from South Louisiana. I know nothing about Arkansas." To this day, Stephen Jones, the guy who now runs the Dallas Cowboys with his dad Jerry, calls me Hip Sled Ed—and we always laugh about it now.

◀ 3

MIAMI

After two fun years in Arkansas, I was home in Larose watching Miami beat Oklahoma in the 1988 Orange Bowl to win the national title. My friend Bill Johnson was there as a graduate assistant with the Hurricanes on Jimmy Johnson's staff. After the game, I called the University of Miami office to congratulate Bill. Tommy Tuberville answered the phone. He was another Miami graduate assistant at the time, who I'd met earlier in the year in an elevator when the Canes came to our place and beat the heck out of us.

I said, "Hey, Tommy, can I speak to Bill?"

"Bill just left us," Tommy said. "He got a job at Louisiana Tech."

I thought fast and said, "That means you have a graduate assistant spot open?"

"Yeah. In fact, we're meeting on it in twenty minutes. You want it?"

"Yeah!" I said.

He called me back in forty-five minutes: "You've got the job."

I said thank you and drove to Miami as fast as I could.

As soon as I got to Miami, I fell in love with the whole vibe of the place. It was football heaven. This was my style. The way Jimmy Johnson ran things made me think, *This is the way to coach.* They ran an aggressive, get-after-it, 4–3 scheme on defense. I'd learned a lot about technique at Arkansas, but the intensity that Miami practiced with blew me away. I'd never seen guys practice with that kind of ferocity.

I learned how to be a coach on the field from Jimmy and his staff. He had a lot of great people around him. Dave Wannstedt was the defensive coordinator and coached linebackers. Dave Campo was the defensive backs' coach. Butch Davis handled the defensive line and Tuberville was the other graduate assistant. Every one of those guys became either a college or NFL head coach later in their careers.

Butch, the defensive line coach, believed in me. He allowed me to coach the players. We had so much talent at Miami—Russell Maryland, Bill Hawkins, Greg Mark, Jimmie Jones, Shane Curry. They knew I knew my technique. My coaches in college had all been good technicians; Bill Johnson and Jerry Arledge were great with their hands. Wally Ake, the defensive line coach at Arkansas whom I'd worked under, was phenomenal. He taught me how to play the run and how to attack the blocking schemes. I learned more pass rush when I got to Miami because Butch knew that well.

Those Miami practices at that point of my life were the hardest I'd ever seen. The players were some of the best guys I'd ever coached. I know I heard a lot of people say that those Miami Hurricanes were renegades, but that was BS to me. They were disciplined. They *loved* practice. They worked their tails off. You never saw a Jimmy Johnson–coached team not ready to play. Jimmy had a psychology degree. He was a master at knowing which buttons to push. The way they practiced was ultra-competitive. Starters were understandably reluctant to leave the field in practice because they worried that their back-ups might never give back their jobs. That was the culture there. Now, those players were flamboyant, but there ain't nothing wrong with that. They had a little swag to them. Actually, a lot of swag to them—but they busted their asses on those practice fields. NFL scouts would come through Miami and tell us that no other team practiced like our team practiced.

◄

The players were giving it all they had, and I wanted to match their intensity in my coaching. Thankfully, it was a good match and an easy transition.

When Ed came in, some guys come in that capacity as GAs—and you can go three years and you're always leery of what they tell the players. We had a close-knit group with Campo, Tony Wise, Jimmy, and me. It was not easy to blend right in. You had to earn the trust of the group to get in that inner circle, but it took Ed no time for us to trust him with how he taught it and coached our guys.

—DAVE WANNSTEDT, FORMER UM DEFENSIVE COORDINATOR

I was determined to learn everything I could. I would sit down and watch how Coach Johnson evaluated and recruited players. I didn't say anything. I'd take notes. Jimmy had the best eye for talent I've ever seen. He had us watching how the kid performed in all sports—not just what they did on the football field. How'd he move on the basketball court? How hard did he compete? How did his teammates respond to him? What did he do in pressure situations? Jimmy was big on change of direction—could a kid turn and run? He didn't want any "stiff" athletes. He was so thorough.

Jimmy had the vision to see where someone's potential was. He'd say, "Hey, that option quarterback needs to be a cornerback." He'd watch a defensive lineman and say, "That's an offensive tackle." He'd watch a safety and say, "That guy's a linebacker." He'd look at a linebacker and say, "I think that guy can be a really good defensive end for us." His philosophy was to move guys up on defense: cornerbacks would become safeties, safeties to linebackers, linebackers to defensive ends, ends to tackles. He wanted speed and playmakers. And he was never reluctant to tell his coaches no, if his gut warned him about a prospect.

He found guys that other people whiffed on. Nobody else wanted Russell Maryland out of Chicago. Jimmy did, and Russell became a star—a great leader and the first pick of the 1991 NFL draft. Larry Lacewell, who later spent a long time with the Cowboys running their scouting department, had turned down Cortez Kennedy in high school when Lacewell was the head coach at Arkansas State. Cortez became a pro football Hall of Famer after turning into a great lineman for us at UM.

I felt like I was getting a master's in evaluating talent under Jimmy. I remember when we saw Warren Sapp in high school. He weighed about 220 pounds, but he was a special athlete with a world of potential. Back then he had narrow shoulders but a big ass and could really move his feet. He'd played quarterback in eighth grade and returned punts in high school. We took him as a tight end, and that's what he played his first year at Miami. Our other defensive line coach Bob Karmelowicz and I recruited him to switch and play defensive line.

One day I got him a sandwich and said, "Hey Sapp, come eat with me. At tight end, you'll catch a few passes a game but you come over to the defensive line and you can affect every play you're on the field." I'm glad he wanted to make that move. We all were. His first step was like no other, how he could shoot out of his stance before the offensive linemen could even move. Sapp kept on getting bigger and bigger, from 245 to 255 to 270. I remember him running a 4.7-second 40 on grass while weighing 285. Incredible. That was Miami football.

In my first game as a grad assistant coaching at Miami, we beat top-ranked FSU, our archrival, 31–0. It was awesome to be part of something like that.

◀

I was only with Coach Johnson for one season. He left to become the head coach of the Dallas Cowboys under his old Arkansas teammate Jerry Jones, and most of our staff went with Jimmy to the NFL. Dennis Erickson came in from Washington State to take Jimmy's place, and he promoted me. I became a full-time assistant defensive line coach, at age twenty-seven, working under Bob Karmelowicz, the defensive line coach. We became great friends. I taught Bob the "43" attack defense, certain techniques Jimmy had taught us, and the Miami way, and Bob was great to me.

We won the national title in 1989. We had the nation's number one defense and set a school record for sacks—fifty-two—that still stands today. Four of our defensive linemen were drafted in the first three rounds the following spring. The next year we finished number three in the country and ended the season crushing Texas in the Cotton Bowl, 46–3. Russell Maryland became the first overall pick in the draft a few months later. My third season at Miami we won another national title, after shutting out Nebraska in the Orange Bowl 22–0. I had a great room of guys I was coaching. We had so many big, fun personalities who you could mold in there—like Dwayne "The Rock" Johnson—and they pushed each other to do better. We were the hottest thing in football, and I was living it up.

◀

I had a trendy place in a high-rise that overlooked the bay on Brickell Key in Miami. My drinking and partying, though, started to get out of control. It became a three- or four-night-a-week deal, staying out late. I couldn't stop drinking, and it led to other problems. I had a false sense of reality. I thought I could stop it on my own, but I couldn't. I tried several times.

I was out of control. I'd gotten in trouble. I was ashamed of that. My boss, Dennis, was great to me. But I just couldn't stop drinking.

I had to get help. In October 1992, I took a leave of absence from UM and never returned. I left Miami and went back to Larose.

I was sleeping back home at my parents' house in my old room that still had my basketball trophies. Those first couple of days back home, I couldn't even get out of bed.

I had fast-tracked my coaching career and had a dream job. I had been recruiting and coaching the best players. We had won two national titles, and I'd blown it all. Everything that I had worked so hard for. Gone. All of it.

This was a different kind of hurt than when I'd left LSU as a freshman when I was eighteen years old. That was more embarrassment. And a kind of shame that said, *Here I go again. How'd I end up here?* But I was reeling from this a lot more. It was a bigger fall because I had experienced success. I had won two national championships. But I had a chemical dependency and couldn't shake it—although I had tried as hard I could. I felt helpless.

But what stayed with me was that every time I went back to my roots, I came back stronger. I didn't know it at the time, but it was because of the guidance of my father and my mother. They taught me what unconditional love was.

I was thirty-one years old, living at home, but they never wavered in their support. One day my dad sat me down on that swing by our home. "Son, take your time. Get whatever you need to get straightened out. I don't care how long it takes. Stay here as long as you like, as long as you need to. Always remember that your dad and your mom are 110 percent behind you."

He had a good way of being a straight shooter, and he could figure out when something was wrong with me and guide me along. We talked about the mistakes he had made when he was younger. I never wanted to let my mom and dad down. They were such loyal people, and a sense of their unconditional love overwhelmed me while I was staying in my parents' house.

◀

I heard about the John Lucas Treatment Center in Houston, run by the former basketball star. How the heck I knew to call the John Lucas Treatment Center, I have no idea, but I'm thankful I did.

I got the number and called there. I told them I was a football coach and had lost everything. The woman on the other end of the phone said, "Sir, do you have insurance?"

"No, I don't. I don't have anything."

"I'm sorry. We can't help you."

Five minutes later, my phone rang. It was John Lucas himself.

"Do you have a ride to get here tonight?"

My daddy gave me a ride to Houston that night. I got settled into the facility the next day. There were some pro basketball players in there with me. My second week there, a famous NFL defensive lineman was checked in. I started talking to him about this tennis-ball drill I did with my defensive linemen that would help his get-off and make him a better pass rusher. He looked at me like I was crazy and started laughing. Even in recovery, my passion for the game never faded.

My time in Houston was life changing. I did all the counseling sessions and went to the meetings every day. They taught you how to live your life without drinking. I realized that it wasn't going to be easy, but I had a lot of people that I knew I could lean on.

I was in the hospital for thirty days and in John Lucas's treatment center for forty-five days as part of their program. John Lucas never asked me for a penny.

I completed the program and returned home at the beginning of the 1993 football season. Again, I stayed at my parents' house—a safe place. My dad told me, "Stay here, get yourself right and your career will come back ten times better than it was. Just do what you need to do for yourself."

I took my dad's advice and stayed put until that winter, when I decided to go to the American Football Coaches Association convention. This is the annual event where thousands of coaches from all over the country gather. When I'd gone there before, wearing my Miami shirt, everybody was my best friend. This time, it was a 180-degree difference. I thought I'd be able to find a job, but I got nothing. All the jobs were taken.

When I got back home I got a call from Henry Lafont, a lawyer in town who was a Nicholls State booster. He asked if I would be willing to volunteer at Nicholls. I said I would. I just wanted another chance to coach football. The next day, Rick Rhodes, the head coach there, called. He offered to let me volunteer. He was the first coach to take another chance on me. He was very good to me. I lived in my old room in my parents' house, with those old childhood trophies around me, and every morning at 4:00 a.m. I'd make the forty-five-minute drive in my mother's old station wagon to Nicholls. On Wednesdays, I'd sleep in the office there. I was the first one in the office and the last one to leave. I was just so happy to be back in a locker room, putting on coaching shoes and getting back out on the practice field.

At the end of my full season as a volunteer coach, a linebacker coach left, and Rick hired me full-time as a replacement. I asked him if I could go out on the road for May recruiting. He said, "Ed, we don't have any money."

I said, "Can you give me a Nicholls State golf shirt? I'll use my dad's truck and pay for the gas myself."

That first day—May 1, 1994—I got out of bed at 5:00 a.m. I hadn't slept much the night before because I was so excited. I had gone over in my head so many times what I was going to tell people when I entered their schools. I thought to myself, *I'm selling Nicholls State. I don't have to make excuses.* I knew I was lucky to have that job. I didn't feel like I had to say anything about how I used to coach at Miami or how I had transitioned from being with the University of Miami Hurricanes to the Nicholls State Colonels. I was home down on the bayou, and there were a lot of people I knew. I respected what Nicholls had done for me. I was more than happy to sing their praises out on the road.

That morning, my mom noticed that I couldn't stop smiling. She asked why I was so happy.

"Because I'm gettin' the greatest gift," I told her. "Today, I get to go out and recruit."

So I took out my daddy's green Chevy S-10 every day, going from high school to high school. I loved it. I was back out on the road, recruiting in the state of Louisiana. I had to take some big steps back to regain my coaching career, and one of those steps was to prove that I could still go out and recruit. I didn't realize it at the time, but that recruiting process meant a lot more than just trying to reel in some prospects. It was also that competitive fire. I was on the chase, all while trying to battle in my recovery. It cleared my mind and helped me feel like I was becoming the man I always wanted to be.

I knew we had to get great players to have a championship team. I saw how much recruiting mattered when I was with Jimmy Johnson at Miami. I dove into it, and I loved seeing the coaches and getting to know the mamas and the daddies. I loved finding and connecting with under-the-radar guys like the Mike Pattersons, the Kenechi Udezes, the Dexter McClusters, the Justin Jeffersons, and the Joe Burrows. I was finding diamonds in the rough. It's a little like reeling in that big fish, only by building relationships and trust.

When it comes to changing your life and being brutally honest with yourself, that is where the magic is—when you turn bad things rooted in weakness and make them into a strength. People always knew I had a wild side, and it came out when I drank. That did it to me. There was always a part of me that was fairly normal, but when

I was drinking, you couldn't really tell what was inside. Channeling the passion and energy that was tied to that wild streak—and having the discipline to control it—has become a great asset for me in coaching and in connecting with people.

The whole competitive aspect of recruiting gets me going. It's about reading people, trusting my instincts, making connections, developing relationships, building trust. And you know that other coaches and programs are all trying to do the same thing. More than anything, I just flat-out love going out and meeting people. I love going into homes where you can see people who need help beyond just football, and you can give them that help.

I know my challenges with addiction will always be there. I learned in counseling that I will battle that until the day they bury me. There were times in the nineties when I thought I had overcome my demons, but then things spiraled out of control again. So now I know it will always be there. When you go through something like addiction and those really trying times—especially when you have children—it motivates you to never allow yourself to end up in those situations again.

It's all about being truthful with yourself. When you're young and going fast, you think you have everything figured out. You think everybody is your friend. Then, all of a sudden, something bad happens in your world and you realize how lucky you are to have three or four real people in your life.

◀

While I was coaching at Nicholls in the Southland Conference, Bob Karmelowicz and Sonny Lubick, two of my old colleagues from the Miami staff, really stuck by me. That winter Bob asked me if I was going back to the coaches convention. He said Syracuse had an opening for a defensive line coach and that he had recommended me to the head coach, Paul Pasqualoni.

The job interview took place in Coach Pasqualoni's hotel room during the convention. He was in what looked like a two-thousand-dollar suite. I was up there in blue jeans with a jacket on, and I was throwing chairs around in that place, going over D-line techniques and gap assignments. When I got back home to Larose, my momma said someone from Syracuse had called and that I had a ticket to fly up there in the morning. They hired me the next day.

I started immediately. The job paid about $60,000 a year. I was so damn appreciative that Coach Pasqualoni took a chance on me at that time. I was broke. That year that I had off, I sat on my front steps and thought about everything that had happened. I'd gone from being a two-time national champ to hitting rock bottom. I remember promising myself that when I got a chance to climb back up the ladder, I was going to hold on tight to each rung and appreciate that climb—because my first time on that ladder, I'd sprinted up it. I went to Syracuse with the mindset that I was going to work my ass off.

I was so impressed with Coach Paul. I learned about his zone blitz schemes and how smart he was. He could coach any position. He was ahead of the curve in doing junior recruiting. We never did that at Miami, but Syracuse was doing that because Penn State had started doing it.

Coach Paul didn't have the talent we had at Miami. He was always looking for an edge. We had to out-coach them and out-scheme them, and most of the time, we did. He was a fair, good man. He worked long hours, and so did his staff. When we got to work, our hair was on fire all day. He won a lot of games—and the way he did it was by outworking people.

In my second season at Syracuse, we had a chance to make the Orange Bowl—but we had to get by Miami first. We committed five turnovers and lost by a touchdown, so we were sent to the Liberty Bowl instead. We headed down to Memphis for Christmas to play Houston. One of the coaches I'd worked with at Nicholls State, David Saunders, who had since moved on to Arkansas State, had been trying to set me up with his friend Kelly for weeks. The timing never seemed to work out, but since we were in the area for the bowl game, it finally did. Kelly and I went out three days before the game and then again the day after we beat Houston. Two months later, we got married. We had a family—Kelly, myself, and her son, Tyler, who was five at the time. A year later we had our twin boys, Cody and Parker.

I'm still amazed at how that all came together. If I'd never left Miami, I would have never been at Nicholls to meet David Saunders, and then if we had gone to the Orange Bowl instead of the Liberty Bowl, I probably would have never met Kelly—and I would never have had my boys Tyler, Cody, and Parker. And then, I probably would never have met a man named Brian Kennedy, who helped save my life.

◄4

FIGHT ON

I had been at Syracuse for three seasons when I got a call from my buddy Bob Karmelowicz, who I'd worked with at Miami. He said he had recommended me to the new head coach at the University of Southern California, Paul Hackett. Paul had coached with "Karm," in Kansas City with the Chiefs. Karm's word helped get me the job at USC. Our twins were thirty days old when we got to Southern California.

The USC Trojans had been struggling. They hadn't finished in the top ten in almost a decade, which was about the same length of time it'd been since they'd beaten UCLA. During my three years on Paul's staff at USC, we went 19–18. The talent level just wasn't there. We had some misevaluations. We had good coaches, but it wasn't a cohesive staff. I learned a lot about myself personally and as a coach in those years though. I'd still had some ups and downs battling alcoholism.

My AA sponsor told me I needed to get another sponsor in California. I'd been reluctant. I didn't want to tell anybody my business in Los Angeles. But I was really struggling. I went out on a Saturday in mid-February—I still remember the date, February 19, 2000—and I came home late after a day of drinking. My boys were two years old, and when they saw me I will never forget the look in their eyes. It was the look of fear. That was enough for me. I never wanted to see that look on their faces again. I realized I needed more help.

When I first got to USC, I'd gone to a boat party in Newport Harbor for our coaches, put on by Don Winston, a USC fundraiser. All the coaches were there, along with some prominent Trojan boosters. Brian Kennedy was also there. At the time, Brian was just a USC fan who had graduated from USC in the sixties. It seemed like everyone was drinking there except Brian, and that stuck in my memory. Two years later, I went to another USC function; Paul Hackett had a golf tournament at Mountain Gate Country Club. It was a really hot day. I was in the locker room getting cleaned up after riding around in the golf cart all morning. Everyone was going to get drinks. I'd just met USC legend Anthony Munoz and was having a lot of fun. I started thinking, *Why not me?* I was pretty caught up in the camaraderie and all, and having beers with the boys seemed like a good idea at the time. I bent down to tie my shoe, and for whatever reason I glanced up, and in the mirror, I could see Brian Kennedy behind me, staring right at me in the reflection. I didn't know Brian well at the time, but I remembered him from that boat party a few years earlier.

He just knew something was wrong. I guess I just felt him looking upon me, sensing I really needed help. He asked me what was wrong.

Ed said, "Can I talk to you? I noticed when we were on that boat, you didn't drink." I said, "I don't drink anymore, Ed. Believe me, I have had more than my share." He said, "I think I have a drinking problem." The standard answer of AA is, if you think you have a problem, you probably do.

—*BRIAN KENNEDY*

Brian had been sober for thirty years at that point. I asked him how he'd done it. He told me he had a desire for living. Then I asked him if he would be my sponsor, and he agreed.

"You got to make me one deal, though," Brian said. "Before you take a drink, you have to call me."

I agreed with that. I wasn't going to go against my word. And that changed my life. I called him every morning at 7:00. He answered the phone. Every time. I'll never forget that. He was always there, which was critical for me.

◀

Things had been shaky with our program at USC. Many top local recruits were leaving LA. The year before the top two in-state players went to Miami and Florida State. Shaun Cody was my big recruiting focus in 2000. He was a local defensive tackle from Los Altos who had just been named the *USA Today* National Defensive Player of the Year. His daddy, Mike, was a huge Notre Dame fan, and Notre Dame had torn us up that year.

That Sunday night our offensive coordinator, Hue Jackson, called me up and asked what I was doing the next day. I told him I had a home visit with Shaun Cody. He said, "Nope, we're getting fired."

He was right. Well, sort of. USC fired Paul Hackett. The athletic director, Mike Garrett, then told us that nobody else was fired, and they were going to let the new head coach see who he wanted to keep. He said, "You can either start looking for new jobs or you can go out recruiting." Brian Kennedy, my sponsor, advised that I get out on the road and recruit. So I did. I was at Cody's high school by 9:00 a.m., about ninety minutes after I heard they fired Paul.

A coach from Colorado was also visiting the school that day. He asked, "What are you doing here, didn't ya'll just get fired?" I said they fired Hackett, not me. Then, I went to a high school in Valencia and ran into a coach from UCLA. I heard him say to someone while looking at me, "What is he doing here? He ain't even got a job."

It didn't matter to me. I called our recruits every day for two weeks. I went to Shaun Cody's playoff game and I ran into his daddy in the stands. I extended my hand. He wouldn't shake my hand. He had the recruiter from UCLA on one side of him and a coach from Notre Dame on the other, and they all laughed at me. Mike Cody looked at me and said, "You don't have a job and you don't have a head coach."

I was steamed. Before I walked away to go down to the sideline, I said, "Listen, I'm going to coach at USC for as long as I want, and I am going to coach your son."

I kept thinking about what had just happened. I started to feel sorry for myself. *You know what, they're right. But why should I take this crap? Why am I letting those coaches laugh at me? Screw this. I am not gonna let any man laugh at me!*

I wanted to go back up into the stands to confront them but thought better of it. I said to myself, *You'd better get the hell out of here.* So I got back in my car and drove away, furious.

I just started driving, not knowing where I was going. My phone rang. It was Barry Sher, the defensive coordinator at Los Alamitos High.

"Hey, where are you?"

I didn't even know where I was in Southern California. Barry used to come to a lot of our practices and watched all of our techniques. He told me I had to see these juniors at the Long Beach Poly game against Loyola. It was at the Anaheim Angels Stadium.

I looked up. I couldn't believe it, but I saw I was coming up on the exit for Anaheim. That was a sign—true as day. I pulled in.

It was a foggy night around 10:00 p.m. I walked onto the sidelines, and I saw Pete Carroll coming toward me. I'd actually met him at the beginning of the season. He was with Carl Smith when we played against Penn State in the 2000 Kickoff Classic in New Jersey. Pete was out of coaching that year. Carl had recruited me out of high school for a school that used to be called Southwestern Louisiana. They worked together at the Patriots and at NC State in the early eighties. He and Pete had sideline tickets, and Carl brought him over to me. "Bebe, I want you to meet Pete Carroll."

Pete came up to me. "Eddie, hey, what are you doing here?"

I said, "I'm recruiting."

"For who?"

"For USC."

"But y'all got fired two weeks ago, right? What are you doing?"

"I've been out on the road recruiting." I told him that the AD at USC said the new head coach would decide who he was going to keep, and I'd just been doing my job.

"Do you know some of these guys?" Pete asked.

"Yeah, that's Darnell Bing over there. That's Herschel Dennis. That's Winston Justice. That big tight end is Mercedes Lewis. And that big D-lineman is Manny Wright." I asked, "What are you doing here?"

Pete told me his friend had brought him to the game. And that they were naming him the head coach at USC on Monday.

"Well, Coach," I said, "I am recruiting Shaun Cody, who is the *USA Today* Defensive Player of the Year. I'm going to be there at his school at 7:00 a.m., and I want Shaun Cody to be the first recruit you talk to. This is a must-get guy."

"Okay," he said, "here's my number. Don't give it to anybody."

That Monday morning, I went to Shaun Cody's high school. I called Pete and put him on the phone with Shaun. Before Shaun hung up, he said Coach Carroll wanted to talk to me again. Pete told me, "Hey Eddie, we got a press conference at two o'clock, I want you to be there."

At his press conference, I saw most of the assistants I hadn't seen in two weeks. We went into the little staff room. I took a seat way in the back of the room. Pete told the group, "I know we got a lot of good coaches in here, but I'm not keeping anybody."

My jaw dropped. As we all walked out, he stopped me. "All except you, Eddie. Let's go to work."

We jumped into a heavy two weeks of recruiting, and got to know each other really well. We kept chasing Shaun Cody. Nobody thought we were going to get him. Everyone assumed he was going to go to Notre Dame.

I wasn't giving up, because I knew Shaun wanted to come to USC. He knew the players I helped develop at Miami. I had a strong connection with him. I convinced his dad, Mike, to come on a visit, and then Mike and I walked the pier in Manhattan Beach. We mended fences. He said, "You know what, Coach, I think I can trust you."

The night before signing day, Pete and I slept in the office at USC. We must've tried calling Shaun Cody fifteen times between his home line and his cell. Pete was worried we weren't getting him because we hadn't been able to talk with him that night. I wasn't sure. It seemed odd.

The next morning, I called Shaun's house again at 7:00 a.m. Big Mike answered.

"Hey Mike, how's Shaun?"

"Didn't you hear? Congratulations, Coach! You got him!"

That was huge. Getting Shaun Cody, the top defensive lineman in the country, was a big statement for USC and for Pete, since he'd only been there for a couple of weeks. In the previous few years, FSU, Notre Dame, and Michigan had been plucking the best players out of California. Keeping Shaun at home wasn't just a signal to those other schools that things had changed—it was a signal to all the local recruits too.

Pete made me his recruiting coordinator and asked me what

areas I wanted to cover. I told him I wanted Orange County, where I lived, and the Valley, because that's where that UCLA coach recruited. I never told Pete why I wanted the Valley, only that I promised to dominate that area. I don't think we ever lost another recruit to UCLA from there. Two years later, we signed nine of the top ten ranked players in Southern California. I knew something special was happening there.

Shaun started as a freshman, but he tore his ACL. I went to see him in the hospital, and saw his mom and dad. Big Mike came to talk to me with tears in his eyes. "Thank you for convincing me to let my son stay home. I couldn't have taken it if my son got hurt at Notre Dame and I couldn't have been with him." He and I ended up being best friends. Shaun recovered and went on to make All-Pac-10 twice and became a consensus All-American and the Pac-10 Defensive Player of the Year in 2004.

My dad always wanted me to go to Notre Dame. Ed Orgeron was so passionate in trying to get me to come to USC, though. The night before signing day, we had a family discussion, going back and forth. And then my dad was all in. After that, I'd gone to an awards presentation in Chicago and I'd talked to some other recruits from around the country. They were like, "You could go anywhere. Why are you going to USC? They're not winning. What's the draw there?" But I just had that gut feeling I got from Ed Orgeron and Pete Carroll about the direction of the program.

—*SHAUN CODY*

And we were glad he did take a chance on us. We were both in for a life-changing stint under the leadership of Coach Pete Carroll.

◀ 5

PETE'S WAY

◀

About a month after Pete had been hired, he held a team meeting at the Coliseum at midnight. I thought, *What the hell are we doing?* The lights were all on. He didn't tell anybody what was going on. He pulled out a big rope and challenged the team to matches of tug-of-war. Linebackers versus running backs. Defensive backs versus wide receivers. Offensive linemen versus defensive linemen. Coaches versus coaches. Everybody was pulling for their unit. The linebackers and defensive linemen were cheering on the DBs while the offensive line and running backs were cheering on the receivers. Then, Pete asked us all, "Who won?"

"Guys, when we're pulling against each other, nobody wins," Pete said. Then, he had everybody get on the same side of the rope and pull. He said, "See how easy that is when we all pull together?" After that, he called everybody to come to the fifty-yard line, line up back to back, and get in real close.

"Listen up, everybody," he said. "If we can stay this close together, we will win every game we play in this place, and we're going to win championships—but we have to stay this close and always pull together."

It was a powerful lesson. That sent a message to everybody there that night and made them realize the power of a team as opposed to just being individuals. Before at USC, we'd all seen a lot of "It's not my fault. It's your fault. It's his fault." It was every man for himself. Guys came to USC just to try and get to the NFL—not necessarily to play on a team. I saw it.

That was the number-one thing Pete changed. He gave us the

motto "One team, one heartbeat"—and I've used that as a guiding light ever since.

◀

Pete had a great way about him that people took to. He gave everybody that warm fuzzy feeling. Pete made it fun to come to work, made it fun to come to practice. Guys believed in what we were doing—in what we wanted. He brought so much positive energy. It was fun, but it was serious too. He made us love to compete; he cranked it up, whether it was in nine-on-seven drills at practice or one-on-one drills between receivers and DBs, or in one-on-one pass rush drills between offensive and defensive linemen.

Pete had another motto: "You're either competin' or you ain't." That is who he is. I figured that out from our first day together in recruiting.

Jimmy Johnson was similar to Pete as a leader, but Jimmy was more stern. With Pete, you rarely saw that side. Pete was a lot looser. He was always a nice guy, but after practice, when we watched the film, he was serious about the little details and making sure we got those things fixed. He would embarrass you if your five-technique got reach-blocked by the offensive lineman. I would get sick to my stomach if I saw that happen at practice, because no one wanted to let him down. Pete knew how to use his staff, and he knew how to motivate us.

Each day of the week had its own specific focal point. We started the week with "Tell-the-Truth Monday," and that meant we were going to be brutally honest with what we saw on film from the previous game. The film doesn't lie. Good, bad, or indifferent, it didn't matter—as long as we were telling the truth. A lot of times, some coaches will sugarcoat things, or they'll just yell at their guys. This was all about shooting straight.

Next came "Competition Tuesday"—that meant full-pads, good-on-good, going as hard as we could to make each other better. Everything was posted in the meeting rooms the next day and graded by Coach Carroll in the meeting. If you did well or had a rough day, you knew it was going to be shown on that big screen in front of the entire team.

Then, on "Turnover Wednesday," our defense strove to force turnovers, and the offense was all about ball security, because they knew we were coming for them. Strip attempts were measured; so was ball security. Everything was charted, including tackles for loss (TFL). If the defense forced at least three turnovers for the day, that was a win for us. If we didn't, the offense won. Pete wanted to see at least eighteen to twenty strip attempts by the group.

Thursdays were "No-Repeat Thursdays," which meant having your mind sharp and no mental mistakes as the game plan came together. It was our dress rehearsal.

Fridays didn't have a nickname. When I took over at LSU, we started calling it Focus Friday. But at USC, every Friday Pete pulled out a big bass drum and beat it. He got the idea from one of our coaches, Kennedy Polamalu. Players would come into our offices at Heritage Hall in between classes to hit it. You'd hear that around the building, and it was like a signal: "We're primed and ready to go."

I never knew where Pete came up with the idea for our daily scheduling, but I always thought that was something I was going to do when I became a head coach.

◄

That first season with Pete, we started 2–5 and he never blinked. When we lost to a Notre Dame team that was 2–3, Pete asked, "Eddie, what do you think's wrong?"

I told him I just thought it was going to take a while, and that we weren't very good yet.

He replied, "I refuse to believe that. We are good enough. We're going to start winning. I'm not going to let my mind go that way." And he was right. We had lost four of those games by five points or less. We ended up winning four of our next five games, including shutting out number twenty UCLA, 27–0. Pete was incredibly strong mentally, and consistently positive. He would not believe what other people said. He didn't read the newspaper. He didn't listen to talk radio. He told us not to read the stories people were writing about our team. "It will give you false reality," he said. "They don't matter. We matter. We control our own destiny."

Of course, I realize it is one thing to say that and another to actually do it, since human nature can be a pretty strong lure. When I was the head coach at Ole Miss, I read everything people wrote about me and my team, and it pissed me off. I later learned better.

After his first season at USC, Pete sent Lane Kiffin and Steve Sarkisian, who were on our offensive staff, to visit with Jon Gruden to learn the West Coast System, with all its slants and sluggos (routes). He brought in Alex Gibbs from the NFL to teach his zone-blocking scheme, and we changed our offense. Carson Palmer, our quarterback, came out of nowhere to win the Heisman Trophy that season and we went 11–2 and finished number four in the country, crushing number three Iowa in the Orange Bowl, 38–17.

Recruiting was going great. We became the hot school in college football, and it didn't take very long for most people to forget that Pete had once supposedly been like USC's fifth choice for the head coaching job. Before he'd been hired by USC, Pete was fired by the New York Jets, and then let go by the New England Patriots after three seasons.

He would talk to me a lot about "nuggets." When we were out riding around recruiting, he'd say, "Hey, Eddie, I'm gonna give you a little nugget." Or sometimes, he'd pick a topic—"Come here. I'm going to teach you how the free safety should read the post." He taught me how to play the intentions of the quarterback. He passed on all sorts of wisdom that he'd learned along the way from his experiences and all of the books he had read to better himself. He was training me to become a head coach; showing me that you have to constantly evolve, even when you think you've matured. "I didn't realize what type of coach I was going to be till I turned fifty, Eddie," he once told me.

Pete was a big affirmation guy. In my first year with him, I had to drive his Mercedes one day. It was sunny out, so I took the visor down and an affirmation card fell out. It said, "I will be a disciplined coach today. I will coach this team firm." I guess it might have been because some people around the NFL had said that he was soft.

He wasn't, though. Once you crossed the line with him, there was immediate accountability.

He and I had a great balance, and we knew we'd taken on good cop/bad cop roles with the team.

"Eddie, you get on 'em, and I'll love 'em up."

I didn't mind it. It came naturally for me. I was the defensive line coach. I'd run the weight room for a little bit. I'd been the discipline guy. The guys understood they were not going to cross me. Pete wanted me to be the bad cop when I needed to be. Sometimes, I pissed him off when I went a little too far.

He always had a plan. He brought a lot of intelligence to it, and had a high standard of performance. "We're the Trojans," he'd say. "We are going to be elite." He found his ideal way to push people and get them to be at their best. "Hey man, is that all you got?" He brought the NFL to the college game.

It felt like a yin-yang deal between me and Pete. In all the areas where he was really strong, he was able to help me. He helped me calm down and not be too aggressive. He knocked some of the rough edges off of me. He told me that I didn't need to be the defensive line coach my whole career. He gave me the opportunity to be the recruiting coordinator and a special teams coordinator and an assistant head coach. And then, in all the areas where I was really strong, I was able to help him. He needed a big man with a presence to help him set the discipline structure, and he needed somebody strong in recruiting. I had done all that stuff before.

> You knew when Coach O walked in the room, you sat up straight in your chair, you made sure your hat was off and there was no fooling around. I remember coming back to USC after I went to the NFL and thinking how lax the place was without Ed around. It was a totally different vibe.
>
> —*SHAUN CODY*

Pete was the most instrumental guy in my career that I coached with. I looked up to him. I'd have died on the sword for him, and he knows that. There were some bumps in the road, some disagreements, but I loved working with him. We won the national title in Pete's third season at USC and then went undefeated in 2004, his fourth season there. About three weeks before we played undefeated Oklahoma in the Orange Bowl for the national title, I was named the head coach at Ole Miss. It was the end of an era for me.

In the Orange Bowl that year our guys dominated on both sides of the ball against Oklahoma. We shut down their great running back Adrian Peterson. We were leading 38–10 at halftime. We won 55–19, giving the Sooners the worst bowl beating in OU history. USC won back-to-back national titles and had won twenty-two games in a row. An incredible way to go out. The day after the Oklahoma game, we were on the road to Ole Miss.

Before I left, Pete's wife, Glena, came over and gave me a big hug.

"Thank you so much for what you've meant to me and Pete," she said as she broke down and cried. I was incredibly touched. It was an honor to have meant a fraction to them of what Pete's leadership meant to me. He had made me believe I could be a head coach, and I was about to road-test that training for the first time.

◀ **6**

| | | | | | | | | | |

THE NFL LIFE

I started out my time at Ole Miss wanting to put into practice all the things Pete taught me, adding my own ideas. But, in actuality, I didn't have the trust in the people around me, the discipline, or the resources that Pete had at USC. After I was canned by Ole Miss, it lit a new fire under me. At the beach with my family in Destin, I began to sort some things out. I picked through my past and identified where I needed to grow, things I needed to bring back into practice, and things I needed to let go. With this transition, I wanted a new challenge. It felt like this was the ideal time to go away from the world of college football for a bit and get a different perspective on the game.

In late January 2008, when college football was all about recruiting and getting ready for signing day, I planned to go down to Mobile, Alabama, for the Senior Bowl. That's where everyone in the NFL—coaches, scouts, GMs, agents, and prospects who had just finished their senior year in college—convened for a week. It turned out that I was the hot prospect.

On Monday morning I drove to Mobile in my Hummer, not knowing what to expect. I figured I'd meet some people and say hi to some folks. But Sean Payton, the New Orleans Saints head coach, called me on my way there.

"Hey—you're my first order of business," he said. He asked to meet me for lunch and talk about possibly becoming their new defensive line coach. We met up at Wentzel's Oyster House, where a lot of deals in the NFL get done the week of the Senior Bowl. We had a good visit. I'd grown up a big Saints fan, and my connection to the team had only grown since my buddy Bobby Hebert had played there. I told him I appreciated what he was doing for the state of Louisiana. He didn't offer me a job but just said we'd talk later. And from there, things took off like wildfire.

During the week I got wind that an old colleague from my USC days, Kennedy Polamalu, who had become the running backs coach of the Jaguars, had been pushing them to consider me for their D-line job in Jacksonville. When I went to the Senior Bowl practice in the afternoon, Larry Lacewell, an old friend who had spent a long time working with the Cowboys, called me and said Dallas wanted to meet with me.

"Jerry Jones wants you to have dinner with him tonight, at Wentzel's."

So I went back there that night and ate in the back room at Wentzel's with Jerry, his son Stephen, who I'd coached at Arkansas, and Wade Phillips, the defensive coordinator.

I had a good time with them. I didn't know the Cowboys were going to come after me like that. They offered me the job right there at the restaurant. I was honored that the Cowboys wanted to hire me. The Dallas Cowboys were a big deal, and the lure of that was pretty strong. They were America's team. Everyone who is a big football fan grew up watching them. Tom Landry. The star. Jimmy Johnson won Super Bowls there. Wade is an excellent defensive coach, too, so working with him was appealing. That all would have been great, but I'd talked things over with my family. My kids wanted to move back to Louisiana and be near their grandpa and grandma. I thought about it, and just felt something calling me to come back. I had grown up a big New Orleans Saints fan and I knew I could learn a lot from Payton because he's such a smart coach, but this was really a family-driven decision.

I went to find Sean. I told him the Cowboys had just offered me a job. "But," I said, "I want to come to the Saints." He said, I had it. "You're offered right now."

That all happened in less than twenty-four hours. I called my wife and my family, and Pete Carroll, and I accepted the job that night.

◀

It seemed like everything had happened in a whirlwind, but really a lot had been going on behind the scenes to get me to that point. First of all, someone stepped up for me and was instrumental in me going to the Saints: my old player Cortez Kennedy. I'd coached him at Miami and we'd stayed close. Mickey Loomis, the Saints general manager, had been with him for years at the Seattle Seahawks. Cortez was like Mickey's son. He got me the job.

Cortez had also been like a son to me. Even after we both left Miami, he would always call just to say hi and see how things were.

Cortez had come to Miami from junior college. I remember that first day of camp in his first year, we had all of the guys running 110-yard sprints in gray cotton shimmels, or half-shirts. He was all of 350 pounds—maybe 370. It was a scorching hot day in Miami and we were a month from playing Florida State, who was number one in the country.

That first 110, Cortez beat every other lineman we had and let out a big "Whoooo!" The second 110, he won it again. The third 110, he beat everyone again and then ripped off his shirt and started swinging it in the air.

"FSU! We're gonna whip their butts!"

Everyone was in awe of him. And then, we ran a fourth 110, and he passed out.

Trainers had to come get him. I think all Cortez did that first season was play on the field goal team. He got the nickname "Two-play Tez."

That was the year Jimmy Johnson left for the Cowboys. Tommy

Tuberville and I were the only holdovers on defense. Cortez would always come into my office saying, "Hey Coach, how's your mom and them doing?" One day he asked me, "What do I need to do to play here? How much do you need me to weigh?" He was probably around 340 at the time.

I said, "Cortez, what are you going to do if you don't play pro football?"

He told me, "I'm going to be a state trooper back in Arkansas."

I said, "Cortez, there's not a big enough police car in Arkansas to hold you. You really need to get down to 285."

Cortez and I got really close. I always had confidence in him, and I think that was what made us grow closer. Because he wasn't in shape, he got tired easily. He had to learn how to play, but I knew once he got in shape, he could be special.

That summer he roomed with Randy Shannon, a linebacker and one of our smartest players. Randy put a lock on the fridge and ate every meal with him, and I think he slept in the kitchen to keep Tez from snacking after midnight! He even took his car keys away so Cortez couldn't sneak out. Randy took him under his wing and really motivated him. Up at dawn, they'd run three miles. At noon, they lifted weights. At dusk, he'd run some more. Cortez started getting a little more confidence as the weight started to come off. He really wanted to be good. He got down to 295 by the beginning of the season and nobody could touch him that year. He was always a great kid and a big teddy bear. I'm grateful for him helping get me back to Louisiana.

Curtis Johnson (CJ) also played a big part for me. He was the Saints receivers coach and was really close to the head coach. CJ and I had worked together in Miami and I knew he also went to bat for me to get it done.

◀

I was nervous during my first meeting of camp with the Saints. Sean started out by saying, "Here's what I wanna tell you guys. Listen—it doesn't matter how you got here, whether you came here as a first-rounder, a fifth-rounder, or a free agent. It doesn't matter if you've been coaching here thirty years or this is your first meeting. You're here now. Do something about it. Let's see what you're going to do with it. Let's go!"

That was a great tone-setter. Sean's meetings were always short, and they always had a clear message and were very precise.

Sean ran everything crisp and fast in practice. I thought he was a great coach. The thing that I learned from him is that people are always trying to find out how we're practicing and specifically how we prepare. I realized in the NFL you don't go to your scout team to work. The rosters are half the size of what you have in college football, and the margin of error in practice is so small, things must be exact—precise. I learned that with the Saints, and I demand that at LSU now. You can't afford to have any sloppiness or some learning curve that's going to muck things up in practice.

After I saw how that worked in New Orleans, I said to myself, *When I get my chance to run a program again, it's going to be first-team offense versus second-team defense*. We were running ten plays, and they had to be exact in how we execute them. And it was a friggin' battle. Then, second-team offense versus first-team defense. You're getting good against good. How many times in college did we try to get Pork Chop, the fourth-team offensive guard, to pull around on the power play, and he just couldn't get there fast enough? Now, if you're using your second-team guard in there for it, who was fighting for playing time, it just looked a lot different because everything is in the details—you really need to replicate the speed of what they are going to see in the game. Look—Pork Chop's probably a great kid, but he never got there because he just moved too slow. And we don't get better as a team because of those little (big) details. That was such an eye-opener.

When you rep it like the Saints did, you keep getting better and you get the speed of the game. When I took over at USC, we had such a limited roster numbers-wise because of the NCAA sanctions, I said, "Screw it, this is how I'm going to do it," and ever since then, we've been doing it that way.

I also learned at the beginning of LSU's season in 2019 how that "scout team" label can also be something you have to overcome. We'd made a mistake with it when somebody got smart and wanted to put the opposing team's jerseys on 'em. It all just went to crap.

Uh-huh.

I didn't want our guys feeling some kind of stigma, like they were embarrassed to be seen as scout-team guys and they didn't want to get reps like that. Like it was beneath them. We took those jerseys out and went right back to them feeling like it's first team against second team—and our practices picked right back up.

After getting a close-up look at the Saints offense and how their quarterback, Drew Brees, operated it, I could see it was certainly different from anything I had been around in college. The Saints ran some "21" personnel—with two running backs and one tight end—like we did at USC, but it just seemed so much more aggressive. Brees was always attacking. Two things stood out about that system: one, it was all about getting players in the space and letting them make plays; and two, I really loved how Sean Payton was going to take eight deep shots per game, two per quarter. Sean's offensive philosophy was, "You gotta tell them—the other team's defense— that you're coming after 'em. You gotta loosen them up and make 'em be honest." That set everything else up. I figured out that when I got another chance, this was the kind of system and mentality I wanted on offense.

◀

Coaching in the NFL was a big change for me. When I first got there, the defensive linemen in the room had to see what I was made of. I got challenged in the meetings, which was good. They knew I knew my stuff. But I didn't connect with all the guys.

I felt like in college ball, I knew I could connect with most of my defensive linemen. My value to them in the NFL wasn't as high as it was to my college guys. There, I didn't just teach them but helped develop them as people, as men.

In the NFL, I think some of the guys felt they were above me. I realized pretty early on that the players were going to decide whether they were going to allow me to coach them or not, and some wouldn't. I knew how much more I enjoyed college football than the NFL. I really missed the personal relationships. In college football, I am more like their father. That doesn't happen in the NFL. Plus I really missed the recruiting—the chase—and building those bonds with the parents and the kids.

Going to the NFL did give me a much better perspective while allowing me to fade into the shadows a bit. After you get fired, your ego is a little bruised. Hopefully, you're working to figure stuff out, to get yourself better. I had to figure out what I wanted to do. I didn't want to *not* coach. The NFL felt like a job to me. In college, I couldn't wait to go to work. The NFL felt redundant. I was treated well by the Saints and Sean Payton, but my role as a defensive line coach was minimal. I was essentially the head coach of the defensive line and nothing else. I didn't want to just be a defensive line coach. I'd grown out of that.

Being in Louisiana for my family was great, especially with the way the NFL workweek was structured. I got to see my oldest son, Tyler, play on Friday nights. I got to see my twins, Cody and Parker, play on Saturdays. When I had some time off with the Saints, I cooked for the kids and their teammates. I really loved that time with my boys and their friends. If we were going to eat at 5:00 p.m., their friends showed up at 4:30. We'd all be in the backyard with my boys and five or six of their buddies, and I'd grill for them and we'd all hang out. When I was at Ole Miss, I didn't get the chance to do anything like that. I said to myself, "Man, if I treat my team the way I treat these kids, they'll play well for me."

We had a good staff in New Orleans. It was very professional. But on the field, our team struggled. We had a bunch of injuries on defense. Drew Brees did throw for over five thousand yards and was the NFL's offensive player of the year. I got to study his work ethic every day. He was impressive. We finished the season 8–8, but we'd lost six of those games by five points or less.

About a month before our season ended in New Orleans, Lane Kiffin got hired as the coach at Tennessee. I knew Lane wanted to bring me to Knoxville to be on his staff. He'd been sending me boxes of orange Tennessee gear. Around the same time, Les Miles was trying to hire me at LSU. When LSU was in Atlanta playing in the Chick-fil-A Bowl, one of Les's staffers, Ronnie Haliburton, stayed behind and gave my family a tour of the facilities. I was still a bit apprehensive. I'd always wanted to come back to LSU. I just wasn't sure it was the right time. My kids got to go out onto the field and tour the stadium. They got to put on LSU helmets. When I saw that, my blood started pumping. This was the first time my family had been inside the locker room at Tiger Stadium. They were wild about it.

When our season with the Saints was over, we took a family trip back down to Destin. Lane Kiffin and his dad Monte surprised me by flying down there to recruit me. Lane knew Les was trying to hire me to LSU, so he came down to pitch me on the Tennessee Vols. I've got to give Lane credit. He was the one who really upped the assistant coaching salaries in college football. He said, "Come be my assistant head coach and come work with Monte." He offered me $650,000 a year. I respected Lane. I really did. When we worked together at USC, he was a hell of a coach. The other big factor was that I loved the 4–3 defense. I had always wanted to work with Monte, who was the Godfather of the Tampa 2 scheme, and learn his defensive system.

When I got back to Louisiana, Les Miles flew back from the bowl game and met me in a Chili's parking lot in Destrehan. He really did a good job recruiting me. He'd come straight off of their team bus. He was serious. If I went with him, my family could stay in Louisiana. I was torn after I talked to him. I felt like a recruit again. He was going to pay me the same money as Lane. He said, "Just think about it and give me a call tonight."

I didn't want to have to leave my family. I lay in bed that night thinking about it. At about midnight, I texted Les a number—$900,000—the same amount I had been making at Ole Miss as the head coach.

Les didn't get back to me. I had to be up early to leave the house by 5:00 a.m. to get on a private plane to fly to Tennessee. Lane was smart. He knew LSU was coming on hard.

When I landed in Tennessee, I got Les's response. He agreed to the $900,000.

I wanted to back out on Tennessee, but I couldn't. I'd given Lane my word.

Kelly and I came to look at homes in Tennessee. But after we talked, I felt like I was going to be with Lane for one to two years and become a head coach again, so we decided, why move the family again? They would stay in Louisiana, and I would stay in an apartment in Tennessee and commute.

◀7

WORKING
FOR LANE

Lane did a good job of recruiting an excellent staff. Obviously, getting to work with Monte was huge. I ran recruiting and handled the D-line. He got Jim Chaney, Eddie Gran, Frank Wilson, James Cregg—these were some of the best coaches in the country at what they did. As a group we had a lot of energy.

When I started recruiting for him that year, I didn't know how valuable Atlanta was until he put me there. Recruits and their high school coaches were buying in. Our players were too.

Everybody seemed to be buzzing about Tennessee that year from the time Lane took over. Some of the stuff Lane did and said ruffled a lot of feathers. Some of the things were overexaggerated, but there were some things that were out of control. I think those things would have had to subside if we'd stayed there long-term. My experiences there were limited. I'm sober. I wasn't going out and drinking. I basically was around the football offices, out recruiting, or back at my apartment.

I went there to become a head coach again. I'd spend all day with Monte. He treated me like a head coach. He treated me with respect. I learned a lot from him about how to coach. Monte was a big tips-and-reminders guy, a big PowerPoint guy, very detailed. Everything had to be neat and precise. On Fridays, I'd fly home to Louisiana to be back with my family.

A lot of our guys really improved when we got there. I had a defensive lineman, Dan Williams, who had gone there as a three-star recruit, worked his butt off for us, and became a force in the middle of our defense. He left UT as a first-round pick. Dan was a really good player. Our quarterback, Jonathan Crompton, went from being a big question mark to one of the better QBs in the SEC after working closely with Lane and Chaney. We also had a lot of future NFL talent.

We ran the heck out of the ball. We played good, solid football. We were competing with people. We hung with number one Florida in the Swamp when everybody was saying how Urban Meyer was going to embarrass the Vols after some of the things Lane had said in the off-season. They were a thirty-point favorite and ended up winning, 23–13. We opened the season 2–3 with two close losses to Auburn and UCLA and then blew out Georgia, 45–19. We had number one Alabama up next in Tuscaloosa. Coach Nick Saban had Bama rolling at that point. We were a big underdog. We held them to about 250 total yards and no touchdowns, and outgained them by about 100 yards. Our kicker was lined up for a forty-four-yard field goal with four seconds left to win the game, but Alabama's nose tackle burst through the line and blocked the kick. They won, 12–10.

These near-wins gave our team a ton of confidence. They knew we were improving. We whipped number-twenty-one-ranked South Carolina the following week. We finished the season 7–6, and everyone around the state seemed pumped up about the direction of the program.

It was cool to be a part of Tennessee football. The Vols treated us well. They loved us and gave us all of the tools we needed. They opened the doors for us. Peyton Manning, the most famous Vol, welcomed us. They all believed in us. It's a really good football school with such a passionate fan base and a rich tradition. I enjoyed seeing what the program meant to people in that state. I felt that if we would have stayed there at Tennessee, we'd have won the SEC East in a couple of years and become a powerhouse. I really believed that. I think Lane had everything in place. Hindsight is twenty-twenty, of course. Lane probably should have stayed there.

But it turned out we didn't stay in Tennessee for long.

◀

I was back with my family at home over Christmas break when Lane called me. He was in Orlando for the 2009 AFCA coaches convention.

"Hey, we got the USC job!"

"What?"

"You want to come?"

"What?"

I didn't know Lane was going to get the USC job. But it turned out, Pete Carroll had just left USC to become the head coach of the Seattle Seahawks.

It was a no-brainer for me to go back to Southern California. I'd always wanted to go back, and had hung on to the good times we had when we'd been there. I thought we were going to do things the way we did them last time.

I had found out that me coming back to USC was part of the deal for Lane to get the job there. It was contingent that me and Monte had to come. They were going to pay me a million a year. I had to take it.

Everything came together so fast. I think I got Lane's call around 1:00 p.m., and I was on a plane from New Orleans to Los Angeles by 5:00.

I was the first one to get there. I went and met Brennan Carroll, Pete's son, at Pete's beach house in LA. Brennan had been our tight ends coach before I left USC for Ole Miss. We talked about recruiting and all the things we needed to do.

The Trojans had fallen off a bit before we'd gotten back there. They'd gone 9–4 the previous season and got blown out by Stanford and Oregon. Before that, Pete had had seven straight seasons of top-four finishes. They still had good talent. When we got settled in there, we started hearing more about the NCAA investigation that had been going on there related to the Reggie Bush case. Nobody around there seemed to know much about what was going on with it. I'm not sure if anyone was that worried about it. USC was in a tricky spot, and we didn't know what was coming.

We went through spring ball, and we'd kept hearing the NCAA was about to announce what their sanctions were, but there were so many false alarms. Then in June, it all came down: we received a two-year bowl ban and they were taking away thirty scholarships. It was a lot heavier than anyone at USC was expecting.

Our attitude was, "We're not going to let that affect us." But it really did. The fact that we couldn't go to a bowl for two years and were not able to compete for a championship really put a damper on things.

That first season, we finished 8–5 with blowout losses to Oregon and an unranked Oregon State team. Lane was very diligent in his work. I think he had matured from some of his mistakes at Tennessee, but with the sanctions, it was an uphill battle there. We had a good quarterback in Matt Barkley and some talented receivers.

The next year, 2011, we played a lot better and went 10–2. We beat a really good Oregon team up at their place, and one of our two losses came in triple overtime to number four Stanford. I felt like in our third season there, we were on our way and were going to take off. Barkley had opted to hold off on the NFL and announced he was coming back for his senior season. We had eighteen starters back, and we were eligible to go to a bowl game again; but our scholarship numbers, because of the NCAA sanctions, had really dwindled. We did not have much depth. Still, we were ranked preseason number one in the polls.

Unfortunately, we had a hard time getting out of our own way. We opened the season 6–1 but then fell apart, losing five of our last six.

In retrospect, I don't think our ideal culture had arrived yet inside the program. We had dissension among the team, as well as some dissension among the staff. We had changed to practicing in the morning. That sounded good at first, but it felt like everyone was working around the clock. Our special teams meetings were way too long. Guys were tired. Maybe some of the practices were too hard, too long, especially since we didn't have the right number of bodies out there with all the scholarship hits. We wondered if we were starting to wear the kids out. We could feel the decline.

I was the assistant head coach. I've got to take the blame for some of that. Everyone's belief in what was going on inside the program started to diminish. I was worried about losing the team.

When you're an assistant coach, you overhear a lot more stuff around the team than you do when you're the head coach, and I overheard a lot of it: "They don't care about me," and "Man, we're practicing too long," and "He's wearing us out, man."

Guys on the staff were worn down too. They didn't know when to go home. We went from preseason number one to 7–6 and finished the 2012 season unranked.

Being back at USC was a lot different this time for me. My wife and I looked for some homes when we came back. We looked at some places in Mission Viejo, but our kids were going into high school in Louisiana. They didn't want to move again. I lived in the Radisson near USC and my family stayed back in Louisiana. The older my boys got—the older I got—the more I regretted being away from my family. We started Skyping whenever we could. I talked to my wife two or three times a day, but I still felt distant from my kids. That was hard on all of us. I wasn't sure how much longer we could stay apart. Something had to give.

◀8

FLIPPING THE SCRIPT

USC fired Lane one month into the next season. We had lost to an unranked Washington State team at home in week two and then got crushed by an unranked Arizona State team, 62–41, in late September. We dropped to 0–2 in Pac-12 play. I found out they were firing Lane right before we took off to fly back to California from Arizona.

Mark Jackson, one of the associate athletic directors at USC, told me on the tarmac that they were naming me the interim head coach.

I took a deep breath and cursed.

It was a bittersweet deal. I didn't want to see Lane fired. I didn't want that, because I was a part of it. But then I started thinking about it. *Well, here comes my chance.*

The next morning when I got up, it had begun to sink in. *You're given this opportunity. You've got to take full advantage of it.*

He sent me a text that morning: "Today, I get my chance, son." That was it, word for word. It damn near brings a tear to my eye now. Just talking about it gave me chills. I still get 'em when I think about it. From that moment, nothing has ever been the same. He then texted, "I'm running with it."

—CODY ORGERON

When I took over, we had a bye week before playing Arizona the following Thursday, so we had a little extra time to get adjusted.

The number one thing I wanted to do was change the mindset and the vibe around the program.

I was determined to flip the script on everything. I promised myself, *I am going to get these kids feeling good about themselves.* I knew most of the players and their families. I had recruited half those kids.

I had been keeping a notebook of everything I had learned along the way from the time I left Ole Miss. I kept it on my nightstand in the hotel room I'd been living in since I'd come back to Los Angeles. One thing was clear: it all started with me, treating my players as my kids.

If I'd have gone in there and come at them hard, doing the same stuff as Lane, and done it just like how I did it at Ole Miss, it wouldn't have worked. The results would have been pretty similar. I'd been thinking a lot about that. I believed in my heart that I was ready.

> He really changed his whole demeanor once he took over. He let us be with our families. The way he talked to the staff was real calm. He listened to what we had to say as position coaches, and let us coach. It was completely different from what a lot of people expected he'd be like.

—*JAMES CREGG, FORMER USC OFFENSIVE LINE COACH*

We had been having a lot of longer practices, two hours-plus. I changed that immediately. I shortened practices. I wanted to get their energy and their spirits up. On Mondays, we practiced in just shorts and a jersey. No pads. We practiced almost half as long as before—but, because the players knew practice was shorter, they understood that we wanted them to go faster. They needed to be more concise, more focused. And they committed to that. They loved it. They knew I was going to take care of their bodies.

From my time with the Saints, I knew how to manage with a smaller roster. I knew the benefits of going good-on-good. Our roster wasn't anywhere near the size of the teams we were playing every week because of the NCAA sanctions. It was more the size of the Saints.

The margin of error when you practice like that was very small. You've got to challenge yourself and set a high standard, right down to drawing up the cards for practice. It had to be perfect.

I knew scout team reps usually were terrible. I wanted it "good versus best available." Otherwise you were practicing bad habits and trying to get good at being bad. Our third- and fourth-team guys got their reps during practice in individual periods, during one-on-ones or in pass-rush drills. Everything else, though, needed to be good-on-good.

Instead of forty plays of service team, we got down to twenty. Those plays were going to be graded and critiqued. The staff knew that if we drilled it, we filmed it—and if we filmed it, we watched—and if it was broke, we fixed it. That was how we worked to get better.

We got rid of the music that was blaring during practice. Lots of programs crank up music while they practice. I thought that was a copout. That's false energy. When that music is blaring, nobody has anything to say. When we practiced at USC, I wanted us to create our own energy. We either clapped or ran, and it was a lot easier to clap than run. Now, at LSU, we've taken that energy at practice to another level. I demand it. Practice has to be game-like.

At our Wednesday team meetings, we had Keynodo Hudson, who was a quality control assistant from Florida, do what we called Key's Fish Fry. At the "Fish Fry" we'd watch videos of our D-line one-on-ones from Competition Tuesday, and Keynodo would bust their chops—but in a good way. He really made it fun. Everybody loved it, and it also helped hold guys accountable. And it was hilarious. He'd put in bloopers from practice, a coach falling over or getting wiped out in a pile-up. He would find stuff from guys' Facebook pages, pictures the players took of each other, coaches' film when they played in college.

It was like Def Comedy Jam and ESPN mixed together. We'd photoshop guys deep-frying in a restaurant with my head on everybody who was cooking the fish. I knew what he wanted. It was a healing; an opportunity to allow them to have fun again. When you think of USC when Pete Carroll was there, it was glamorous, tradition, fun, special. That's what Coach O was bringing back.

—*KEYNODO HUDSON, FORMER USC QUALITY*
CONTROL ASSISTANT

I was determined to flip the script for the team in every aspect, including the things they ate. I wanted them to feel good about being around the football building and about being around their teammates and staff. Lane had taken away the candy bar and the ice cream sundae bars on the away trips. He didn't allow desserts on the training tables. They had to eat a lot of bland foods, like Lean Cuisine and turkey bacon.

I knew he meant well, but the guys were getting out of the facility and going to Burger King and McDonald's at night. When USC upgraded their facilities, they created a fancy dining hall with the idea that all of the student-athletes and the staff would eat together and develop some camaraderie. But with the foods we'd been allowing them to eat, it had become counterproductive.

My first night as the head coach, we served them all fried

chicken and ribs, and we had cookies. I think they ate about five hundred cookies that night. Other sports teams came over to eat with us. They got to take little bags of cookies back to their dorms. Everybody on campus loved me for that!

We still wanted them to get good nutrition, but we eased off for the sake of morale. I got rid of that turkey bacon. We catered in dinner from Roscoe's Chicken and Waffles. I surprised the team one night with In-N-Out burgers. I had the coaches go eat dinner with the players who weren't in their position groups, so everyone got to know each other better when their guard was down and they were more relaxed.

The coaches had been staying in the office until midnight. I told them to go home and get out of there by nine at the latest. Wednesday night became Family Night, time for the coaches to take a break and relax with their families. On Friday nights, I took them to the movies. I remembered that legendary USC assistant Marv Goux told me he used to take the team to Paramount Studios. So we went on a little field trip, and they got to see a movie before it was released. I knew the guys appreciated that. Leonard Williams, our great defensive lineman from Florida, told me after the movie premiere, "Thank you. I'd never seen this stuff since I'd been here, and this is part of why I had come to USC."

Practices had been closed to the media. I opened them back up. Just like when Pete was the head coach. Lane wasn't discussing injuries with reporters. I provided details about our injury list daily. That was completely the opposite of how I handled it at Ole Miss. I was going to throw them some sugar and kill them with kindness.

The media had been good to me when I was with Pete at USC, but it was a different story at Ole Miss. Back then, I read everything the press wrote and got angry about it. And it affected me. There was some ugly stuff. The mocking hurt. I didn't know how to handle it. But at USC, I buried the sword with the media. Today, I'm stronger. They gave me some internal motivation.

You can't fight the media. Now, I give them everything and I'm as honest as I can be. I learned from Pete.

◄

My first game as USC's interim head coach, we arrived at the Coliseum about two hours before kickoff. I led the team through the colonnade entrance, which was what we had been doing as part of our "Trojan Walk" out onto the field on game days. But, I wanted to surprise the players. Normally, the players' parents would line the way to the Coliseum, but I'd told them not to do the Trojan Walk this time.

As we made our way in, a lot of the kids were looking around, confused—"Where are my parents?"

Then, when we got near midfield, near the USC logo, they realized all of their families were sitting there on the field waiting to give them big hugs. They were all smiling and their hearts were swelling with pride. I gathered everybody around in a circle around the USC logo and led them in a chant of "One team, one heartbeat." Then our running backs coach, Tommie Robinson, led us in a prayer. The whole thing was very powerful.

When it was time for the game, Keyshawn Johnson, wearing Ronnie Lott's number 42 jersey, led us out of the tunnel onto the field. Earlier in the week I had brought out another USC great, Marcus Allen, to speak to the team. I am grateful for Marcus, who has become a big supporter and an excellent resource for me. I hoped bringing all of those Trojans back would provide great motivation.

Arizona came into the game 3–1. We jumped all over them. We led 28–3 in the second quarter and got our first Pac-12 win of the season. It felt good to see the players happy in the locker room.

Regardless of the good start, I didn't feel I was a real candidate for the USC head coaching job from the beginning. I was made to feel that way. USC had just moved into our new offices in the McKay Center, and Lane's office was gorgeous. It had a balcony that overlooked our practice field across the street. But I was told I should keep using my assistant coach's office and to only use the head coach's suite when I had to, like when I was talking to a recruit. I was uncomfortable whenever I was in there, because I might run into Pat Haden, the USC athletic director.

At the beginning, Pat had been really good to me. He was a former starting quarterback at USC, and had grown up around the program. One of his best friends growing up was J. K. McKay, the son of John McKay, the legendary Trojans coach. I think Pat always had me pegged as just an assistant coach and never thought I was worthy of being the head coach at USC. I believe he liked me as an assistant coach, and as a recruiter, and as a person, but that he didn't think I was cut in the mold of being USC's head coach.

◀

We lost the next game at Notre Dame, 14–10, but then bounced back to beat Utah 19–3, and then went up to Oregon State and hammered the Beavers 31–14. It was USC's first win up there in almost a decade. The team carried me off the field after the game. At that point, I felt like I could be the head coach of this program and it had become *our* team.

We followed that up by routing Cal on the road and then hosted number four Stanford, the most physical team on the West Coast. USC hadn't beaten them in five years. They were a tough matchup for us because we were so limited in numbers. We only really had one backup player on defense to rely on the whole night. That was asking a lot of our guys, but they responded. The biggest play of the game came on a fourth-and-two with a little over a minute remaining. Cody Kessler, our quarterback, connected with Marqise Lee for a thirteen-yard gain on a slant pattern and helped set up our kicker Andre Heidari for a forty-seven-yard field goal. He nailed it. Our guys delivered in the clutch. We won 20–17, holding Stanford to its lowest output of the season. It was USC's first win over a ranked opponent in two seasons. We had a sellout crowd in the Coliseum. They stormed the field for the first time in fourteen years. I got to go up on the ladder and lead the Spirit of Troy, our great marching band. It was a magical night in the Coliseum.

After beating Stanford, I felt like I deserved the job. I also knew that the more it became my team, the more Pat Haden, who was trying to conduct a coaching search to land a big name, didn't like it.

The next week we beat Colorado on the road to go to 6–1 since I took over. We moved up to number twenty-three in the polls—the first time we'd been ranked since the night we'd lost to Washington State in early September. All we had left in the regular season was our rivalry game against UCLA. They were number twenty-two in the country.

I had a meeting with Pat Haden the day before the UCLA game. He told me that he was 99 percent sure that I was going to be the next head coach at USC. We had talked about a deal at three million dollars a year. He had the contract all made up. He had it on his desk, but he didn't sign it. It felt disrespectful the way he dangled the job in front of me.

But then he introduced me to some people as the next head coach at USC.

"I've just got to make it a formality on Sunday," he said. "Tell your wife to stay over to Monday. Make sure you've got some suits."

I brought my family out for the UCLA game. My boys flew in from Louisiana.

◀

The game kicked off at 5:00 p.m. Haden had called me in the hotel earlier in the day, which was odd.

"You know this is a very important day for you, Ed Orgeron," he told me. I had a really bad feeling about it. I was thinking, *You've already told me that I'm going to be the next head coach.*

I think he was under a lot of pressure to hire me, and there was something inside of him that didn't want me to win that game so he could pull out. At least that was my feeling. But I'd taken his word for it that he would call me on Sunday and offer me the job.

We were a little off Saturday night against UCLA. We were fired up before the game. I don't know if we were trying too hard. I had an eerie feeling all week that we wouldn't stop their quarterback, Brett Hundley. We didn't have a good game plan for him with their QB draws and their run game. We couldn't slow Hundley down. Our offensive line got banged up in the game. We lost our center early in the game. We struggled to score. We lost, 35–14.

After the game, I knew Haden wasn't going to hire me. I just knew it. Sunday morning, I put my kids on the plane back to Louisiana. They were crying because they thought USC wasn't going to hire me after the loss. I told them, "This is going to be okay," even though I knew it probably wouldn't.

I stayed in that hotel all day long. Haden never called. That man had told me he was going to call me. He never did. I stayed up all night long. I couldn't sleep.

Monday morning, I heard from someone else. USC was hiring Steve Sarkisian for the job. I heard about it from someone else. Not Pat Haden. I was not happy.

Pat and I met later that Monday morning in the head coach's office at USC. It was very intense—probably as intense as any meeting I've ever been in during my career. We met for about thirty minutes.

I told him he was making a mistake. "I am the better hire for USC." I asked him point blank why I was not getting the job. I asked, "Was it because I was never good enough for you?"

He couldn't answer me.

I loved USC. I knew I was the better hire. I felt betrayed—like I was promised something, and he pulled the rug out from under me.

I met with the team a little bit later to say goodbye to them. I took the high road as much as I could.

"Hey men, it's been a wonderful journey," I told them. "This is still a great place." I told them they were still at the best university and that they needed to follow their new head coach. "Tomorrow morning, I am going to bring my kids to school. Something that I have not done in four years. I have stayed in a hotel for four years. I have neglected my family for four years." I told them that I loved them.

It was like a funeral. Every one of the players came to hug me. Some told me that I was like the father they never had. The coaches each came up and hugged me too.

Haden was in the room. His face looked sick, seeing all those kids crying. He had to be disgusted with himself. I don't know how he sat through that meeting with those kids. I think he was the one guy in LA who didn't want me to be the head coach at USC.

To this day, that was probably the worst day of my life. We knew the elephant—we didn't beat UCLA—but when Haden announced it to us, that was terrible. To this day, that pisses me off. I'm sure to this day, after seeing what he's done at LSU, they regret that. We just didn't understand. I know we didn't get certain wins, but the culture was changing and it was going to the way it needed to be. Nobody comes into that situation and is gonna win every game. It really was heartbreaking.

—ANTWAUN WOODS, FORMER USC DEFENSIVE LINEMAN

I just had to get out of there. Nobody was going to convince me to stay. It was such a miserable day. Kelly and I got in our Tahoe and rode off to the airport to fly back to New Orleans that night. When we got on the plane, I told Kelly, "Besides the day I buried my father, this has been the worst day of my life."

She said, "No, it's not. God has a better plan for you."

"Well," I said, "it'd better be good."

◀ **9**

I I I I I I I I I I I I

COMING HOME

When I got home from USC, I was gone. It was like getting over a death for me. My wife was worried about me. My boys were worried about me. I would end up sleeping most of the day on the couch. I was devastated.

I knew he was in trouble. He had saved that USC program like four times. I'd called and called and called, and I couldn't get in touch with him. He would always return my calls. If he started drinking again, there was nothing I could do until he wanted to get back on the program. I've been in AA fifty years and have seen a lot of people—wife left, something happens to the kids, and they fall off the wagon. I was scared to death for him. I know he was devastated. I just had to wait to hear back from him. I was so relieved when he called. He said he was fine and said that he just had to leave town. I told him that you're more important to me as a person than whatever USC has to offer.

—*BRIAN KENNEDY, AA SPONSOR*

After a few weeks back in Louisiana, I had some good opportunities to go back to coaching. Nick Saban had called to see if I wanted to be the defensive line coach at Alabama, and Urban Meyer had asked if I wanted to be his D-line coach at Ohio State. I'd always had great respect for each of them, but I just wasn't ready to go.

I was crushed by USC. I thought I couldn't be any good to any team at that point. That wasn't like me, but I believed that I was right where I needed to be: at home with my family.

I went with my kids to San Antonio to watch Parker compete at the US Army All-American Game Combine. I took a call from a famous USC alum who was willing to pay out of his own pocket to get me to come back, but not as head coach. They were offering me a five-year contract for $10 million guaranteed that would have made me the highest-paid *assistant* in college football. That kind of money was unheard of at the time for any assistant. That was head coach–type money.

> I was on the balcony and my dad came out. He looked at me. He said, "Son, if you don't stand for something, you'll fall for anything. I deserve to be a head coach one day, and I will be a head coach."
>
> —*CODY ORGERON*

It took me about three months to start to get over what had happened at USC. I'd fallen in love with that place. I knew all about the rich tradition of Trojan football. I embraced it. I celebrated it. I felt like I took full advantage of the opportunity, just like I had told my sons that I would when I first heard I was going to become the interim head coach. They wanted it for me as much as I did. It stung knowing that they could see the heartbreak on my face.

That position gave me another chance to rewrite my story. The great thing about life is that no one else gets to define you. It's up to you. What "they" say, what "they" think, isn't important. What you *think*, what you *do*, is what really matters.

I understood that. I believed that with all my heart. But I was in a funk for a while because someone, the person in charge at USC, didn't think I was good enough. And I knew he was wrong.

I'd never seen facial hair on my dad before. He started looking kinda scruffy when he was back home. He was so hurt. That dark cloud, that gut-punch feeling lasted some months. Later on, he played those voicemails about those job offers. I asked him why he wasn't taking those jobs. He said, "Family means the most to me. No job offer can take that away from me." I thought about that and was like, "Damn, he turned down those jobs just so he could be at our games?" That always meant the world to me.

—*CODY ORGERON*

I think time, going to my AA meetings, going to church, helped me get over it. But the thing I enjoyed the most was getting to go out to my boys' practices. I had never seen them play as they got older. Being back home, I went to every practice, went to every game. I got to be a dad. That saved me.

I started bringing them to school. I'd buy them breakfast. I got back into a routine. I loved working out, lifting weights, then I'd go run by the lake. I'd get them lunch, take a nap, go out to watch them practice, and then grill for them at dinner. I started to love it. It was funny to be out there after being on top of the world at USC in Los Angeles. All of a sudden, I didn't have a job. I'd listen to some of the other parents. They were nice to me, but guys were talking around me, like I worked at the gas station or something. It was kind of funny to see the other side of the world like that.

Parker, one of my twins, had developed into a really good wide receiver, one of the best receivers in the state of Louisiana. Cody was the best tennis player in his class in the state of Louisiana and had won two state qualifying tournaments on the junior USTA circuit. I wanted to embrace all of it and experience as much of it with them as I could. I now had the time—and it gave me a fresh perspective on everything that really mattered to me.

No one in Louisiana really comes to those matches. That first match that he came to—whoa—he is loud. "Yeah! Let's go, Cody! Yeah!" His voice really echoes, and it just carries. I looked at him crazy. "You can't do that here, Dad. You gotta learn tennis etiquette." And eventually, he did. He would even come play tennis with me. I genuinely appreciated knowing how hard he worked at making that connection. Here he was, this big Cajun defensive lineman trying to learn tennis at fifty-two years old.

—CODY ORGERON

I really did try to learn the game of tennis. I took it up because I knew how much he loved it. We would play, but I was horrible at it. He kept getting me with drop shots. One time I really went after one. I pulled my hamstring so bad I never played again. But I had so much pride watching him play. We went to Atlanta, North Louisiana, and Alabama for some of his matches.

I grew to respect the sport of tennis. I saw how competitive you have to be to do well at it. It takes great hand-eye coordination and footwork, and all that work Cody had done on the tennis court really helped him a year later when he joined Parker on the football team as his quarterback. They went to the state semifinals. Cody had a wonderful tennis coach who had also worked with Monica Seles when she was younger. That woman was instrumental in him growing up.

◀

Around April when spring football hit, I started watching interviews with coaches. That got my blood going again. When training camp came, I was running 110s in the Louisiana heat, like I was getting ready to go. My passion for the game had come all the way back by the fall.

Parker had a good football coach at Mandeville High. I was the first one in the stadium for his games and the first one leading the cheers on the third downs. Every Wednesday night I had the coaches and some of the players over to the house. I made steaks for them or catered in food just to give back to them. I let them do their thing in the backyard.

Every night it was like a big feast when we came home from practice. It was a big bonding time. All of our friends would be over, and he was just being our dad. We'd talk about life and school. He was so pumped to come to our games. Like it was his game day. It was dad with no football being home all the time, which we weren't used to at all. But we needed that year so much. We grew so much together. Me and my dad weren't that close before. I couldn't remember my dad being home and being lovey-dovey dad until then.

—*PARKER ORGERON*

On Saturdays, I'd watch every college football game on TV—although it was hard for me to watch USC play. I studied all the coaches and what they did. Getting to watch the SEC so much, I felt like I could compete at that level, and I wanted to stay at home. It just felt like the right thing for me, and for my family.

◀

LSU had a rough season that year. They had lost to unranked Mississippi State at Tiger Stadium, got blown out by Auburn, got shut out at Arkansas, and ended up 8–5 and unranked for the first time in seven years. I figured they were going to make some staff changes. My old colleague Frank Wilson, who I had hired at Ole

Miss, was the associate head coach and running backs coach at LSU. He deserves all the credit for getting me in there. He got me the job of defensive line coach, no question. I guess he felt like they needed some help in recruiting and on the D-line. Les knew I wanted to come in, and somehow, some way, he got it done.

I'd thought I had passed up my chance to get back to LSU when I went with Lane to Tennessee instead of accepting Les's offer in 2009. LSU was the one place I always wanted to be, besides USC. It actually came together very quickly. Coach Miles treated me with the utmost respect. He was phenomenal to me. He'd told me before it happened, "I know you understand my situation. I want to hire you. Just give me a minute." Then, they hired me and defensive coordinator Kevin Steele at the same time.

I was so ready for it. I was in good shape. I had been going to my meetings. I was refocused. Even though it wasn't my dream of being a head coach, it felt right. I thought, *Okay—here we go!*

The first day on the practice fields at LSU stretching brought back some memories for me.

I knew some on the staff were looking to see how things were going to play out, like, *Does he think that because he's an ex-head coach that he is going to try and tell us what to do?* But really, I was just happy to get to coach football and work with the guys. I was happy being a defensive line coach and I was going to recruit my ass off. I couldn't wait to sell LSU.

◀

When I took my year off from work, I promised myself I was not going to sweat the small stuff. I don't think you have to be a football coach to relate to that. For me the "small stuff" is that interpersonal static that crops up in your interactions. You get on people's nerves. They get on your nerves. Then you let it get in the way of doing your job and being at your best. I wasn't going to let pettiness slow me down anymore.

I always say, "Don't go chasing ghosts." I realized I was doing that to myself a lot. It's when you end up following your worst instincts and getting in your own way. I found out when you truly understand yourself and are honest with yourself, you know how to manage things. Then, you can avoid some of the problems that you could have made worse, and make them better instead.

Dealing with resentment and the emotions I had built up inside me was a hard thing to sort out. That is something you learn to work on in the recovery process from AA. I use it as internal motivation. I try to take the emotion out of it. I think, *I've got to work harder.* I just flip it around. Of course, that is not easy. Your own instincts are driving you in a different direction, but you have to remember to be disciplined about it.

I have learned that when you let that resentment and anger stay inside about something, when you think only of what someone else has done to you, it's like you're drinking poison and you expect the other person to feel it.

I didn't grasp that until after Ole Miss and all the ridiculing that followed me there. That took a couple of years to work through. Knowing some media members mocked me—"Coach Oh-no," and their "Yaw-Yaw" jokes—some of that really got under my skin. And it pissed me off for a long time.

When I had the year off, I had a lot of time to think about things. Ron Higgins was a columnist in Memphis who had covered me at Ole Miss. I had been angry about some of the things he wrote about me because my kids read it. I knew they heard the ridicule from the article and from other kids, and because it all happened at such an impressionable age, I knew it hurt them. That really bothered me. I thought it was very unfair.

When I got to LSU, we had a media day. Sure enough, I saw Ron

Higgins, who was on the LSU beat. I hadn't expected to see him, but I went straight up to him.

"Hey Ron," I said as I shook his hand. "I'm happy to be at LSU. I know we had a rough time at Ole Miss. Let's just let bygones be bygones."

"Coach," he said, "I think that we've both matured over the years. Let's have a great relationship at LSU."

And we have. I felt much better after that exchange—like a little weight was lifted off my back. Everybody makes mistakes. When we make a mistake, we always want people to forgive us. Well, what about when people make mistakes against us? There's power in forgiveness.

◀

During my year off, the thing I missed the most was the challenge and the adversity of the daily process at work—having to dig in and get your guys better. There's a scoreboard for it. That stuff makes you better. I missed the 3-technique getting reached, and you got to fix it.

I had figured out what made me tick. Since I was six years old, I'd never *not* been on a team. I was institutionalized in a way. I needed a schedule. I needed competition. I needed practice. I needed a challenge. That's what you get every day in coaching.

Now I could truly appreciate being at LSU. I was more mature. I'd been in the NFL. I didn't come here to compete with anybody on the staff; I just wanted to be a productive assistant and coach my guys. I was happy. After I didn't get the job at USC, and after all that thinking about what might have been, I had to reset my thinking yet again: *I'm just going to bust my ass and let's see what happens.*

I came here to be the defensive line coach. I never truly thought I was going to be the head coach. Eventually, though, things started happening. My mindset was, *Just keep your mouth shut; don't get caught up in the politics.* I'd seen some chinks in the armor around the program, but I just kept on working.

We started the 2015 season 7–0. We moved to number two in the country. But then we had three straight losses by double digits, where we didn't score more than 17 points. After that, we had a week of reports that LSU might fire Les. The team really rallied behind Coach Miles, and we beat Texas A&M 19–7. After the game, the players carried Les off the field on their shoulders and the fans chanted his name: "Keep Les Miles! Keep Les Miles!" Right after that, Joe Alleva, the athletics director, announced that Les would remain on as the head coach.

Before the next season, though, there were more of the same rumblings. We opened ranked at number five in the country and played unranked Wisconsin at Lambeau Field in Green Bay. I knew if we lost to Wisconsin, it wouldn't be good for Les. We lost, 16–14. A few weeks later, we lost 18–13 to unranked Auburn, and we fell to 2–2.

The next day, we had our regular staff meeting at 1:00 p.m. Nothing was said about a firing. It was all the same. We were getting ready for the next opponent, Missouri, who had scored 79 points that weekend. After the staff meeting, I went back in my office to watch film. When I took a break and walked down the hall to go to the bathroom, Verge Ausberry, an associate athletics director, walked up behind me and grabbed me by the arm. I didn't even see him coming. He pulled me aside and said, "C'mon, let's go see Joe Alleva. You're now the interim head coach at LSU."

Joe told me, "You've got full power as the head coach of the LSU Tigers. This is your audition, and I am going to give you a chance. And I believe you can do it." That felt completely different than when I replaced Lane at USC.

We held a staff meeting so Joe could tell the other coaches. He just said that it didn't work out with Les. Then, he said, "Coach Orgeron is now the head coach of the LSU Tigers. He has full power and I'm leaving it up to him to do as he sees fit." I really respected that Joe said that I was the head coach. He didn't say that I was the interim.

I told the staff, "This is a tough time. The team needs us, and we're going to give them everything we got. I am going to make some adjustments. I am going to talk to some of you about that." I brought in Cam Cameron, the offensive coordinator, and told him I was naming Steve Ensminger, who was the tight ends coach, as the new OC. Steve had been the offensive coordinator at Texas A&M and Clemson. Cam handled it well, but he really didn't say much. I brought in Dean Dingman, who had been Coach Miles's right-hand guy, and told him I was making a change with his spot. I met with Bradley Dale Peveto, who had been coaching outside linebackers and special teams, and told him I wanted him focusing on special teams. And then I told Dennis Johnson, who was my graduate assistant, that I was promoting him to become our new outside linebackers coach. Because I'd become the head coach, I now had access to two courtesy vehicles. I gave Dennis the keys to one of them because I knew he didn't have a car and that he had been walking two miles each way to the office, rain or shine.

Soon after, I got a call from Derek Ponamsky, who hosted a radio show in Baton Rouge that I went on every Tuesday morning at 7:30 a.m. the year I was out of coaching, and also did the LSU post-game show.

"Who you gonna hire as your director of operations?"

"You," I replied. "You want it?"

Derek accepted it right then and there. It was one of the best moves I've ever made. He'd become a good friend, and I knew he'd be a big help to me. He knew the ins and outs of LSU. He knew the ins and outs of Baton Rouge. He was very smart and savvy at a lot of things that I wasn't very smart and savvy at. He knew the media; I hadn't been good at handling the media. His communications skills are fantastic. He was a great addition for us at LSU, especially during that transition.

He never offered me a job. He just told me I was getting it, which is a total Coach O move.

—*DEREK PONAMSKY, LSU SPECIAL ASSISTANT*

TO THE HEAD COACH

We sent a text to the players that we had a 5:00 p.m. team meeting. The players were always off on Sundays, so they'd never been called into a team meeting on a Sunday before. By the time they walked in, they knew a coaching change was taking place. Les told the team himself. He said, "Men, they felt like it was time for a change, and I agree with them. You're going to be under good leadership with Ed. I'm always going to be a Tiger. Go Tigers!" As he was about to exit the room, we all gave him a standing ovation.

Coach Miles had recruited that whole team. He had accomplished a lot at LSU, and those players were hurting for him. Les really handled it all like a man, with a lot of class.

I stood in front of the team and told them, "Here's how we're going to do things, and we're going to roll." Then I gave them the tug-of-war deal, just like Pete Carroll did it all those years before at USC. Only we did it right there in the team room. Position groups versus position groups. Even the administration guys, including Verge and Joe, versus the coaches.

"Hey, who wins when we do this? Nobody," I said.

I led everybody, around 150 people, into a long line where we had to double up, but we all pulled that rope together and we did it. I knew they got the message.

> When Coach O got the job, he talked about how we weren't a cohesive unit. We must have the want-to to win together, and everybody had to be on the same page. He started talking about "one team, one heartbeat." At first, we didn't fully understand it; about all eleven men on the field fighting like Tigers; not jogging to the ball, and letting someone else make the tackle. He talked about holding each other accountable— that was something we had struggled with. The tug-of-war was pretty crazy. It gave me chills. I'm not gonna lie, because I felt like everybody got the concept. It made complete sense.
>
> —*CHRISTIAN LACOUTURE, FORMER LSU DEFENSIVE LINEMAN*

Here's what I promised myself from day one after taking over at LSU: *This is going to be my job. And I ain't letting go of the rope.* I didn't say those things publicly, but I swore to say it with my demeanor.

◀10

I I I I I I I I I I I

NO INTERIM
THIS TIME

I swore not to treat my new position as an interim coaching job. This was it for me. I moved into the head coach's office. We had my nameplate put up outside the door: ED ORGERON, HEAD COACH. I let everybody know that I was the head coach there. I wanted to build everything on a foundational attitude that said, "We are going to be successful. Let's go!"

Derek Ponamsky found a picture from when I was a freshman at LSU. I was wearing number 54 on my jersey, and it dawned on me there was some symbolism to that, since I was fifty-four years old when I got the job. I had Derek track down a bass drum for the "heartbeat" meetings I had planned leading up to the games. Luckily for him, Louis Bourgeois in our equipment room had connections with a lot of country music artists in Nashville and was able to get a drum overnighted to us with the graphic "One team, one heartbeat" on it.

Like I had at USC, we changed our practice routine, putting a specific emphasis on each day. We had Tell-the-Truth Monday; Competition Tuesday; Turnover Wednesday; No-Repeat Thursday; and something new we called Focus Friday. The guys immediately bought in to the program and the accountability. I told them, "This is your team, men. You show me leadership and I'm going to give you more and more."

They had been having long, slow, grueling practices. People were tired and beat up. I couldn't wait to change all that, and they were excited about it. We already had a great trainer in Jack Marucci and strength coach in Tommy Moffitt. They had GPS tracking data to help them monitor what the players put out in practice. Jack would let me know, "Hey, they're getting a little tired." Usually, I would I see it before that and back off, throwing them a bone.

> We knew right away that the adjustment was rapid and it was impactful. If you take an average of your players' team speed, and if it goes up .4 or .5 miles per hour in a game, that's pretty darn good. We went up two miles per hour faster immediately. The players were even commenting on it, that they felt so much fresher and faster.

—*JACK MARUCCI, LSU DIRECTOR OF ATHLETIC TRAINING*

Jack and Tommy had told me a stat about how ten of Coach Miles's last fifteen losses had come after Halloween; it seemed the players had worn down and their legs were spent by the final month of the regular season. We had to fix that.

Our practices were much shorter and much more up-tempo. Coach Moffitt's data showed that we had spent 66 percent less time on the field in our first two weeks but we actually only did 25 percent less work, so we were being more efficient in our training.

A lot of times in football, coaches often operate a certain way just because that's the way things have always been done. You end up going down that rabbit hole of trying to work harder, not smarter. I was that way at Ole Miss. Since learning from those days, I was not afraid of finding ways that may be different from the norm, but that worked better for us.

When I took over at USC, I had decided I didn't want our guys waiting at the stadium too long before kickoff. Most teams get over there two to two and a half hours before the game starts. I don't like all that quiet time. That's way too much. Guys lose focus.

I asked our strength coach at LSU, Tommy Moffitt, "What is

the minimum amount of time we need?" He said ninety minutes. So we changed to getting over to the stadium an hour and thirty minutes before kickoff, which I know is about forty-five minutes to an hour less time than other teams leave themselves. I like using the energy we have from our clap session at the hotel, where we play our hype video, and from our Tiger Walk.

It is "tape up, suit up, and let's go." We must've been doing something right, because we weren't having down games.

I also started what I call our Winning Edge plan in our Thursday practices. I was determined to do whatever I could to make sure our team avoided clock-management gaffes and snafus that cost teams so many games.

During a six-minute period at practice—the Winning Edge—we focused on specific in-game scenarios taken from NFL and college games that involved executing a play as the clock ticked down. It could be short yardage, goal line, red zone, two-point plays, when to kill the clock, when to go down—one of our analysts would pull all the film and we'd script it out and rehearse it so everybody was prepared. We made it as real as possible. We practiced going fast on fourth-and-short. We coached them to never stick the ball out when they were trying to cross the goal line because we saw how many fumbles occur in that situation.

I also began to embrace how analytics could better inform my in-game decisions. We started working with a company run by a football coach that provides this phone book-sized, color-coded manual that breaks down every possible situation based on its statistical recommendations tailored to our team and the opponent's tendencies.

While I take everything on a case-by-case basis, I became a big believer in the analytics and the perspective they could bring.

◀

My first game as head coach at LSU we beat Missouri, 42–7. Our new offensive coordinator, Steve Ensminger, called an aggressive game, just like I wanted him to. We put up 634 yards of offense, which was a new LSU record for most yards in an SEC game. I'd told Steve I wanted us to take eight shots a game—two a quarter—just like Sean Payton does with the Saints. With Steve, that was in his DNA, so he was all for it. The next week we beat Southern Miss, 45–10, and then beat number twenty-three Ole Miss, 38–21, hitting on a bunch of big plays. It was also the first time anyone had held Ole Miss under thirty points all season. We were playing with great energy. Guys we knew could play—D. J. Chark and Russell Gage—got more of a chance to make an impact, and they took advantage.

As someone who was not inside the program but around the program, you could see the attitudes just get shot with adrenaline. As good as Coach Miles was, and respected as he was, it seemed as if it got stale. All of a sudden, you could see guys playing for their brother again. It wasn't just a bunch of independent contractors. A lot of these guys had been hearing for years so much about how they were "3-and-outs" [to the NFL].

—DEREK PONAMSKY, LSU SPECIAL ASSISTANT
TO THE HEAD COACH

By the time number one Alabama came to Baton Rouge, we had won three in a row and moved up to number fifteen in the polls. We had lost five straight to Alabama. I was confident we wouldn't back down from them. Our defense really got after them, but we struggled on offense. We looked tight. We couldn't get the running game going. We missed a couple of throws when our receivers were open. We couldn't block them. Their D-line just destroyed us up front. The game was tied 0–0 into the fourth quarter. They made a play on offense, and we didn't. They won, 10–0.

This was no moral victory. I still felt like I had a good chance at keeping the job. We won at Arkansas the next week, 38–10. When we played number twenty-one Florida, I knew that was a good chance to prove ourselves.

We controlled the game but struggled to convert in the red zone. We had two chances from their one-yard line but couldn't get in. We had a fourth-and-goal at the one-yard line to win the game but just didn't execute the play. Our running back went the wrong way and we got stuffed. We lost, 16–10.

I was pretty down after that game. That night my own boys were both playing at McNeese State—Cody was a quarterback and Parker was a receiver—and they had a night game, so I drove over there to root them on. The next morning, I woke up in our hotel on campus, feeling lower than a snake's belly. I was thinking, *Here we go again. We blew it. Man, I've got to get myself going.*

I went into the office. Ponamsky told me that he had talked with Joe Alleva when I was at McNeese the night before. Derek said Joe still felt very optimistic. Ponamsky said, "Hey Coach, we still got a shot here."

That was all I needed to hear. It gave me a ton of energy and enthusiasm. We had a short week ahead against number twenty-two Texas A&M on the road on Thanksgiving night. We had a staff meeting that day. I wanted everyone in our program to feel like we were about to play our best game of the season. I really believed we were. I felt like everybody was watching me. I was fired up as the players started walking into the room for our team meeting—"Hey, let's go! Let's go! Let's go!"

I watched the guys come walking in. One of the last was Derrius Guice, our running back who had been a backup to Leonard

Fournette. Derrius was a phenomenal player. He was a Baton Rouge kid. He had a rough background, and it kept calling him back in the tougher parts of Baton Rouge, but I was never worried about him doing anything wrong off the field. He was a passionate kid. There was nothing too hard for Derrius. He always came to work with a smile on his face. Pound-for-pound, he's one of the toughest players I've ever been around. He was always in the office. He was a team player. He had waited behind Fournette and knew his role and accepted it. To me, he was just as good as Leonard. I knew he trusted me, and I trusted him. Derrius had been the ball carrier who got stopped on the fourth-and-goal and fumbled against Florida.

I saw him walking slowly to the meeting. Head hanging down. Hood over his head. I could see he was hurting. I pulled back his hood and looked him in the eye.

"Son, I love you," I told him. "Put it on me. That's on me. I should've coached you better. Get your head up. I'm giving you the ball this week, and I'm going to keep giving you that ball, and we're fixin' to beat their ass."

He said, "Hell, yeah! Thank you, Coach." He perked up right away. That was all he needed to hear. I wanted to treat my guys just like I treat my sons. That was it right there. It's important for me to show them I care. Show them I have their back. Show them I believe in them. Love them.

I didn't want him to blame himself. We hadn't practiced that play. (It was called Pylon. It was a dive off the left tackle and the tight end was coming across like split zone.) With that play, if he would have faked the dive, that would have sucked up the defense and he would have scored easily. But that was on me.

When I was listening to the play in the huddle, the play I heard was the play I ran. Danny Etling called the play. It was loud. It was crazy. I heard something different than what everybody else heard. When I fumbled and I didn't get in, I was the first one in the tunnel. Normally, after every game, we meet as a team and Coach O tells us how proud he is or how disappointed he is. But after that, he came straight to me before addressing the whole team. "D, you're like a son to me. Keep your head up. This one's on me." He took the blame for everything when I knew it was my fault for not paying attention to detail. And, at that point, with his job on the line, with how I could've really f***ed up his chances of being head coach, and he put everything on him? That spoke more to me than anything, that he wasn't just worried about his job but he was worried about me as a son and as a player. He didn't make everything worse on me than it already was. I was already beating myself up. The next day when we came in, he saw how sad I was. I was still in a funk for sure. "D, that game is behind you. I know what type of player you are. We're going to put the team behind you. This week, I'm feeding you. We're going to let you go off. There's no splitting time or anything like that." After that, you saw a whole 'nother Guice.

—DERRIUS GUICE, FORMER LSU RUNNING BACK

A&M had been playing without their starting quarterback, Trevor Knight, who had been injured—but he came back for our game. We were without our star running back Leonard Fournette, and our star pass rusher, Arden Key. We were also missing our top tackler on defense, Kendell Beckwith. Regardless, it was all about next man up. We decided we were going to be the most physical team on the field. And we were.

We practiced with no pads all week. Duke Riley, our senior linebacker, had become a tremendous team leader for us. When we got on the bus to go to the plane the day before the game, I was feeling good. I knew that we were going to whip their butts. Right when we got off the plane, I saw little groups of people from our coaches and support staff starting to gather. They were whispering about something. I told myself I was going to stay focused.

We went to the pregame meetings in the hotel. The whole demeanor of the staff had changed. The team was fine, but something was off with the staff. I got back in my hotel room. My wife asked, "You heard the news?"

"No, I don't think so."

She said they had offered the head coaching job to Jimbo Fisher. She had gone to dinner, and everybody was talking about it.

I didn't believe they had offered Jimbo Fisher the job. Maybe they had made some overtures to him. I don't know what happened. But I wasn't going to get caught up in those rumors when we had a big game less than twenty-four hours away.

The next day, we were calling our recruits. Nothing had changed on an official level. I wanted to make sure we had a lot of energy, but you could tell that something had been going on. At the stadium, everything was fine—or it seemed like it.

I always felt like Joe was honest with me as athletic director, but there had just been so many rumors swirling. I had gotten really close to Joe's wife, Annie Alleva. I'd learned from a coach a long time ago that you can always tell from a coach's wife how much he likes you.

Before the game, Joe and his wife came over to me. Joe said, "Good luck. Go get 'em!"

I said, "We're going to play great." Then, I looked at Annie and her eyes dropped. She had a frown on her face like she couldn't hide it. I thought, *Oh, s****.

Usually when we win the coin toss, we defer. I had told the whole team the night before the game, "This is what's going to happen. We're going to win the toss. We're taking the ball, and Derrius, I'm giving you the ball."

We won the coin toss. We took the ball, just like I told the team, and we gave it to Derrius. He ran like a wild man. First play from scrimmage, he broke through the hole for nineteen yards. We gave to him the next play. Short gain. Then, we hit a little pass for a first down. Fourth play of the drive. Bang. Derrius hit it. Right up the middle. Four Aggies tried to tackle him. He spun right through them; all of the Aggies ended up on the ground and he was still going. Then, he ran through another A&M player who fell right off of him, and he outraced the rest of the defense to the end zone. Touchdown, LSU! Forty-five yards.

They couldn't stop him. They couldn't stop us. Derrius ran for an LSU record 285 yards and four touchdowns. Danny Etling, our QB, had the best game of his career and carved up their defense. We put up 622 yards on the Aggies and beat them, 54–39. Those 54 points were about the average of what LSU had scored combined for the month of November the previous two seasons. Our locker room was rocking that night after the game. The players were chanting, "Keep Coach O! Keep Coach O!" I'm pretty sure some of the people on LSU's search committee heard it. It felt good.

On the flight home, I still had the feeling something was going on behind the scenes. Derek, who always sat in front of me to the left, had his head down. Someone else came on the plane, one of the support staffers, and said to me, "You did a good job. Sorry to hear about the news."

"What news?"

He said, "They offered the job to [Houston coach] Tom Herman. It was on the ESPN ticker."

I just shook my head and thought, *That's great. Last night, it was Jimbo Fisher. Tonight, it was Tom Herman. Tomorrow it's going to be our turn.*

I knew that Joe always wanted to hire Coach O because of the first couple of weeks and what he'd seen. He knew Coach O inspired people. He's not just a cheerleader. He's a smart guy, an organized leader who was incredibly hip to what was happening throughout all aspects of the program. I figured they're going to interview this guy, talk to that guy, but I knew Joe liked what Coach O was doing. Had we beat Florida, I felt like that week going into A&M, it would have been over with and they would have named him the guy.

That night at A&M was crazy. We're playing a really good game. [LSU sports information director Michael] Bonnette showed me the tweet from one of the Texas reporters [about LSU offering the job to Herman]. I said, "Are you kidding me? We're in this game and this is happening?" But I knew that is not the way Joe operated. Did I know Joe was talking to Herman? Yeah, but I knew for damn sure Joe Alleva wasn't offering anybody else the job while we were still playing, much less on a game day. I honestly believed they were going to give us a fair shake.

—DEREK PONAMSKY, LSU SPECIAL ASSISTANT
TO THE HEAD COACH

Tom Herman had been at Houston for two seasons. He had been a Texas graduate assistant, and it was no secret that Charlie Strong, the Longhorns head coach, was on the hot seat. I'd heard Herman really wanted that Texas job, but it wasn't open yet, and maybe they were trying to leverage LSU to get Texas to open. I was pretty confident Joe Alleva knew I was the best man for the job.

I trusted Joe. I thought maybe members of the board or some search people had gone into some preliminary talks with Herman or his agent, but I didn't believe they had made him an offer.

We were set to meet with Joe at 7:00 a.m. in his office—me,

Derek, and Austin Thomas, who helped in recruiting and was our general manager. Austin had worked on a presentation that we were going to make from a book he had been putting together for three months, outlining everything that we would do to run my program for LSU—how we were going to handle academics, recruiting, hiring coaches and staff, the weight room, media, our philosophy. It was everything from A to Z.

The night before the meeting I didn't sleep well.

In the morning, the three of us were on our way to Joe's office when Derek got a call. Someone had told him, "Y'all are fixing to get offered the job." We were all fired up. We sat down around the table in Joe's office. Derek was to my left. Austin was across from me. Joe was to my right.

I saw the look on Joe's face. His head kinda dropped. It wasn't good. I could just feel his energy. I kicked Derek under the table.

"You guys did a tremendous job for us," Joe said, "but I gotta do what I gotta do. Tonight, I'm going to see Tom Herman."

I immediately asked Austin and Derek to leave.

"Joe, I know that you know in your belly that I'm the right man for the LSU Tigers. And I look forward to being the next head coach at LSU."

I stood up. I shook his hand and looked him in the eye. I can only imagine what Joe was thinking then—*I can't believe this dude just did this. I guess he really does believe in himself.*

The whole meeting didn't even last five minutes.

I called Kelly and told her what happened. Then I went to the Lad Cook, the hotel on campus, and started to pack up all my stuff. But I wanted to keep on competing. I called Pete Carroll and Lane Kiffin and told them to try calling Joe. My plan was to hire Lane away from Alabama to become my offensive coordinator.

I drove out of Baton Rouge and headed toward my family's home in Mandeville. It was going to be the first time in eight weeks I'd be sleeping in my own bed. I got to Hammond, about halfway there, when Joe called me.

"Do you really think Lane is going to come?"

"If he doesn't get a head coaching job, I think he's coming with me," I said.

Joe loved it. I really think that call from Lane helped put it over the top. We were going to run the spread offense and get somebody from Alabama who was a great play caller. Joe thought with my motivation and recruiting ability, plus Dave Aranda coaching the defense and Lane coaching the offense, that we would have the perfect storm.

I got home just in time for Thanksgiving. We had so much food—gumbo and turkey and all the fixings. I couldn't eat, though. I went and sat in the backyard and thought, *Here I go again. What's going to happen?*

Houston had been playing that day and lost to Memphis. Texas lost to TCU. I figured they may well fire Charlie Strong. Tom Herman's name was still on the ticker as coach of LSU. I said my prayers. I looked over at my wife.

"What's wrong?" she asked.

"Look at the TV, woman. They're giving the job to Tom Herman."

She never lost faith. "You're going to wake up tomorrow morning and you're going to be the head coach at LSU."

"Yeah, right."

◀

I woke up at 1:30 a.m. My cell phone was buzzing. I turned it over. It was a text from Lane Kiffin: "Tom Herman leaning toward Texas."

My phone started buzzing again. I didn't get to it in time. It was 5:30 a.m. Missed call from Joe Alleva. I called him right back.

"How the heck you doing?" he asked.

I said, "I'm doing great now that I'm hearing from you."

He asked if I could meet him at 8:30. *Heck, yeah.* I jumped out of the bed. Kelly looked at me and said, "Told you so!"

Joe called me back as I was getting dressed. "Let's meet at 7:30 in your office."

I got in my Tahoe and flew down the road. I was going as fast as I could. I had the moonroof down. I was blasting "Born on the Bayou." But then I started to doubt.

I called Kelly. "Nobody's actually offered me the job."

"Ed," she said, "they're not going to call you to come in to not offer you the job."

I said, "Well, stranger things have happened."

I pulled into the parking lot in front of the LSU football building at 7:29. Joe was standing right in front of the big Tiger by the building.

"So, you want the job or not?"

I ran up and gave him the biggest bear hug I've ever given anyone.

"Will you put me down, you big son of a gun!"

He said, "Ed, I want to tell you something. You know when you said that I knew in my belly that you were the right man for the LSU Tigers? Well, my belly was hurting yesterday."

I said, "I put that Cajun gris-gris on ya."

He just laughed. I don't think Joe ever offered anybody else the job. I always trusted in Joe Alleva to tell me the truth. He was a stand-up man. Obviously, Tom Herman wanting to go to Texas helped. I'm sure LSU vetted some other people, but I am very grateful to Joe. He believed in me when a whole lot of people didn't. He saw me for what I was, and I appreciated that.

◀

I knew Alabama didn't want Lane to leave them and come to LSU as my offensive coordinator. I was talking to Lane throughout that process. He had told me, "Hey, I want to come with you." He knew it was going to help me get the job. And I knew he would follow through if he didn't get a head coaching job. He came close with Houston. Then, we heard about Florida Atlantic University wanting him. He told me he was still coming to LSU but took one more meeting with FAU because he wanted to listen to what they had to say. He ended up taking the job. He was honest with me the whole time about it.

In my introductory press conference after LSU hired me, I still thought we were getting Lane. I overstepped my bounds a little. Obviously, I was talking to Lane, but when that fell through, I felt like I had to get the hottest name out there. To me, Steve Ensminger was the best guy for it. But I ended up hiring Matt Canada who had helped Pittsburgh set a bunch of offensive records. He had a different kind of scheme with a lot of motion and shifts. We knew a lot of other schools were trying to hire him too. My gut was wrenching after I made that hire.

We finished the 2016 season against number thirteen Louisville and their Heisman Trophy–winning quarterback Lamar Jackson in the Citrus Bowl. We sacked him eight times. They went zero for thirteen on third down attempts until deep into the fourth quarter. We held them to 220 yards total—that was over 300 under their average. Derrius ran all over them too, rushing for 138 yards. We ended the season number thirteen in the nation—the highest LSU had finished in five years. We had begun to flip the script in Baton Rouge, but we still had a long way to go. I was living my dream, but I hadn't reached my goal. I knew that we still had an uphill climb.

◀11

FINDING OUR WAY

The way we finished the 2016 season helped set up our national championship team of 2019. We had so much recruiting momentum that we were able to sign a class with studs at almost every position in 2017. Half of our starters from the national-title team came from my first signing class at LSU. We had nose tackle Tyler Shelvin, who was the number-one-ranked player in the state; safety JaCoby Stevens, a five-star from Tennessee; Jacob Phillips, the top-ranked inside linebacker in the country who was also from Tennessee; Patrick Queen, who we thought was one of the fastest linebackers in the country; Grant Delpit, the top safety on our board; Saahdiq Charles, Ed Ingram, and Austin Deculus, who all became starting offensive linemen; Clyde Edwards-Helaire, a great all-around back from Baton Rouge; Kary Vincent, a very fast nickelback; K'Lavon Chaisson, the top pass-rusher in Texas; and then we got a late steal in wide receiver Justin Jefferson.

I think we attracted them because of the positive energy that we had coming out of 2016. We beat Texas to get K'Lavon out of that state. We closed well to get both JaCoby Stevens and Jacob Phillips out of Tennessee. We also had to fight to keep Clyde, who was thinking of going to Mississippi State at the end.

We opened the 2017 season 2–0, beating Brigham Young and Chattanooga before facing Mississippi State in Starkville. We were number twelve in the country. They were unranked. They had lost to LSU the previous two seasons by a combined five points. But they were ready for us.

During my press conference that week, I'd praised their big defensive tackle Jeffery Simmons and said he was so good that we needed to double-team him. Well, he walked onto the field right before the game with his headset on, yelling, "Double-team me! Double-team me!" They were pumped up to play us.

We were not prepared for them. They outcoached us. They outschemed us. And they outplayed us. They had an answer for our 3–4 defense. They were running some plays that we didn't have an answer for. They pulled both guards and were cutting our linebacker. They had a totally different game plan than we had expected. We practiced for QB draws, and they were running sweeps with both guards. They always had an extra player at the point of attack. They were checking everything, and we just gave them the same thing. We made no adjustments. We could have played more of an even front than an odd front. Our offense was stifled too. We had two touchdown plays negated by penalties. We had no plays over twenty-five yards.

They played lights out, and that place was rocking. Those cowbells were clanging. I was so embarrassed at how I had prepared our team. We lost 37–7.

I saw Mississippi State coach Dan Mullen later on somewhere that off-season and complimented him: "Dan, you had a good plan for us." He said, "Coach, we worked on y'all the whole month of June. We had a red-letter game on y'all."

I told our guys after the game, "Hey, put that on me, guys. I didn't get you prepared."

I saw Joe Alleva after the game. He didn't say a word. He looked at my assistant Derek Ponamsky like, *Are you kidding me? Mississippi State never beat LSU like that.*

As rough as that game was, I knew we had to make sure Mississippi State didn't beat us twice. I preach the twenty-four-hour rule. After twenty-four hours, we let it go. When you have a big win, it's tough. You sometimes have to bring them back down to refocus. But our guys know it. That's the point of Tell-the-Truth

Monday. We listen. We watch the film. Then we don't talk about it again.

That Monday I gave them a general overview. "We needed to coach you better. We need to have you in better position. Everybody's going to give you their best game at LSU. I didn't have you ready." We talked about the things we did well on offense, on defense, and on special teams, which wasn't much.

On Tell-the-Truth Monday, you don't look for excuses. It's like when you're young and you get your butt kicked. You just keep your mouth shut and you get back to work. We knew the fans were going to talk about it, so we told the guys to avoid the newspaper.

We returned home to play Syracuse. We ended up in a battle with them. We led 28–26 midway through the fourth quarter. I was shocked that we were struggling like that. I never thought we'd lose the game even when it got tight. The final was 35–26.

You want to focus on winning the game, but when you're struggling the week before, you want to look better. You knew the doubters out there were crushing you. You really feel it.

I just had to stay the course. When I was at Ole Miss, I would have gone nuts after something like that. I would have berated the coaches. I would have berated the players. I would have practiced them harder. But I wasn't going to do any of that. I wanted to show them that it wasn't going to affect me. I was staying the course.

I'd matured since my blow-up days. I was seasoned. When you get fired, a lot of people want to give you advice. I learned that although there are many helpful people, many helpful coaches, I'd better do it the way I feel is best. I need to separate the advice I actually go out and ask for from the stuff people offer up. If my gut tells me I probably should not be doing it, I'm not doing it.

So in the locker room after Syracuse, I told them, "Hey, good win, guys. Way to go!" They needed to hear that. I needed to bring their spirits up. I think they believed in what I was telling them. These guys know I'm going to tell it like it is.

When you're in the middle of it, running a high-profile program, you know all eyes are on you. You're always the tone-setter.

I do my weekly radio show right after practice on Wednesdays. I'm off the field around 6:30 and then the show starts at 7:00 p.m. So after an intense practice I ride from our football complex to T. J. Ribs, a barbecue joint nearby, and over the course of that drive I have to prepare: *Okay. You've got to get your mindset right because they're going to shoot something at you.* It's like switching from being an aggressive coach to being Muhammad Ali and doing a little of that Rope-a-Dope. It is a challenge.

On the weekly radio show after we lost to Mississippi State, we heard from a caller named Terry. He said he had never felt as embarrassed watching an LSU football game since 1981 when Tulane defeated the Tigers, 48–7. I said, "Hey Terry, I hope that makes you feel better." I still remember that call vividly. You just got to take the high road. I think I have taken the high road on almost every call. That's a part of maturity. I understand that I've got to be solid. I can't waver.

The next week, we played Troy. The Sunday before, Joe Alleva, the athletic director, came into my office like he would every Sunday. He said he was starting to hear stuff from the board and some of the alumni. People were worried that we were starting to lose our identity on offense with all of the shifting and motion that Matt Canada was doing with the new offensive scheme. And I agreed with him. We had a true freshman starting at right tackle, Saahdiq Charles. He was a really talented young player, but in that system, we were having him shifting from left tackle to right tackle and back. We were starting two true freshmen on the offensive line, Saahdiq and Ed Ingram. I hated shifting linemen on every play like that. I felt our offense was way out of whack. I told the offensive staff, "This is Troy we're playing. Let's just line up and come after them." By that point, I'd really wanted to go back to Steve Ensminger's offense from the year before.

First play of the game, we had our third-string running back, Nick Brossette, getting the ball. He fumbled. Derrius was hurt. Darrell Williams, our second-team back who we relied on a lot, should've been getting it. They got the ball at our thirty-yard line and scored a touchdown six plays later. We didn't end up scoring a point in the first half. We didn't convert a single third down. We were down 10–0 to Troy.

At halftime, I was with the defense. I think Canada went back to more of the shifts and motion in the second half. We lost 24–21. It was just a terrible performance by us. Troy ran for 206 yards on us. They held the ball for forty-two minutes. Our defense couldn't get off the field. It wasn't like they were beating us with trick plays. They converted ten of eighteen third downs. We went zero for nine on third downs.

The players had that look on their faces after the game that said they couldn't believe what just happened. I told them, "Hey guys, we didn't prepare you well enough. We are going to get this fixed. We're going to have a great week and we will bounce back."

The next day, Joe Alleva came in. He changed his course. He said, "I think we've got to let him run his offense." *Him* was Matt Canada. Joe set up a meeting for Monday morning with me, Canada, and Dave Aranda, our defensive coordinator.

"I just want to let you know that everything's okay," Joe told us. "We gotta get going." Joe always thought that I took too much of the blame, and that the coordinators didn't take enough of the blame. "Matt, you call the offense you want. Nobody's going to get in your way."

From then on, I didn't say a word. I didn't critique his offense.

We barely spoke. It was so awkward. But I just had to get through it. I was told to do it, and I had to respect that.

We had a meeting with our players leadership council in my office right after the meeting with Joe and the two coordinators. I talked with the players for an hour. The guys were very candid with me. At one point, Rashard Lawrence, who was only a sophomore but was mature beyond his years, stood up.

"You were our D-line coach. You were stern. You didn't take nothing from anybody," he said. "I hate to tell you this, Coach, but you've gone too soft on the team. Some of these guys are taking advantage of you. You need to be harder on 'em. Call them out, like you did with us."

I said, "Thanks for telling me that. The other way comes easier to me."

This was a pivotal point in establishing the direction of our program.

◀12

SETTING THE STANDARD

I didn't read the newspapers, but I knew what buzz was going around. I'd heard there was a GoFundMe site set up to raise money to try and get me fired. Everybody who didn't want me hired came out of the woodwork, and they were having fun with it. I knew I couldn't let anything affect me. I wouldn't let anyone see that happen.

At the radio show that week, one caller questioned whether I deserved the job.

I told him straight: "I earned the job, whether you like it or not."

At that time, I wanted to be firm. I didn't want to cross the line. I wasn't going to overreact or offend any fan. I certainly wasn't going to be a pushover, though. At the press conference after Troy, I had to stand up like a man. I thought the media were fair and square about it. We had passed the twenty-four-hour rule, and I had tried to let it go. We had been preparing for Florida for three days, then I had to listen to all of that stuff about Troy. I had reset my mindset on that ten-minute ride to T. J. Ribs. With all the passion our fan base has, when you don't play well, you're going to feel it. But that passion is why you come to LSU.

Each team has its own unique personality. I had to manage the team I had that season. I knew they were reeling. After the Troy loss, I thought, *I'm not going to go hard on them.* Some things I didn't address like I should have or would have liked to—like guys slouching in the meetings or at practice, who didn't seem to be giving it everything they had. I wasn't as demanding like I wanted to be, but I sure wasn't going to go back to cussing and raising hell. I knew we had some good leaders on the team. Christian LaCouture,

Davon Godcheaux, and the D-line were strong. Our center Garrett Brumfield was a damn good leader. Danny Etling, D. J. Chark, Russell Gage, and our tight end Foster Moreau were studs. Derrius was a team guy. I knew I could trust most of the coaches, but we did have some dissension on the staff.

We weren't ready to play Troy. It was like going into a fight with our hands down. The dissension among the staff trickled down to the young men. I think they felt it. A black cloud had come over the team.

Looking back, that game was the turning point of my career. To get things going again, I knew I had to rely on grit and toughness and pull out every ounce of energy I had. I knew I had enemies in the building. My back was against the wall. At that point, I just had to leave the offense alone and make sure we were playing really good defense and special teams. We were going to lean on the guys I knew I could lean on.

In the locker room, it didn't feel like it did at Ole Miss. The team knew who I was. They knew I wasn't going to let anything affect my relationship with them, regardless of the circumstances. It was just like a family.

◀

We were 3–2. We'd fallen out of the top twenty-five. We had to go visit the Swamp. The Florida Gators were on a three-game winning streak. The week before the game, we experienced a turning point as a team. Duke Riley, one of our former players who had been instrumental in me getting the job, came back to visit the team. Duke had been having a good rookie season with the Atlanta Falcons and they were on a bye week.

He came by midweek to say hi to all of the coaches. I asked him if he wanted to talk to the team. He said, "Let me see what's going on and I'll talk to you tomorrow." So Duke took some time to hang around and observe. When we went to eat in the cafeteria, he was in there. He was talking to the ladies who help serve the food, talking to the people who clean the trays. He was out at practice, eyeballing everything that was going on.

After practice ended, he came over to me. "Coach," he said, "I'm ready to talk to the team."

"Okay, Duke. The floor is yours."

"Ya'll know who I am," he started out. "I run with y'all. I'm going to keep it real with you. I've been watching you. This ain't LSU. Who are you freshmen, not picking up your trays after ya'll eat?! Who do you think you are? I'm watching you, defense! You're not running to the football?! Coach O can't take the blame for everything. This is not LSU. You're LSU, and this—*this*—is *not* LSU!"

If you know Duke Riley, he's a light-hearted, kind, funny guy to be around. I don't think we were prepared for one of our friends, an NFL guy, coming back to pour his heart out. The year before we had so many superstars. We had [Leonard] Fournette, Jamal Adams, Tre White, Derrius Guice, but Duke was our team MVP. He let us know that he wasn't cool with us at that point, or with the brand of LSU football that we were playing. He told us the way we were playing was bulls***. That was shocking for a lot of the guys. It wasn't some rah-rah stuff.

—*FOSTER MOREAU, FORMER LSU TIGHT END*

That talk changed my team around. Duke called them out. He saw someone parking in the handicapped spot. He called him out in front of everybody. Called players out for not wearing their gear properly. He stood up and put it on them. Every eye was on him. He talked about accountability. Taking responsibility. They respected

Duke. He was a real team captain. One of the toughest guys who has played at LSU. He came after them as players. He was pointing, screaming, cussing—getting on them for not picking up their trash in the parking lot, thinking someone else was going to pick up after them. At that time right there, we had leadership, but we didn't have a stand-up guy on the team who was going to challenge his teammates to be excellent. That was probably the most effective speech I've ever had from anyone who has talked to one of my teams.

At that point, I don't think I could have talked to them like that. They might have thought, *Coach is blaming us. Here we go.* I've seen so many coaches lose their teams like that.

I think Coach's instincts are right. He might have lost that team if he'd been the one speaking to them like that. The core group of that team, from that 2015 recruiting class, was our lowest-rated character class we've ever had here in terms of our character score on them. I think they would have said, "He's putting the blame just on us." That was the uphill battle. You had to will your way with them because that's who you were playing with. But with that speech, it was the messenger. The beautiful thing about it was, he talked to 'em like a coach. It was everything you want to say but you can't.

—*JACK MARUCCI, LSU DIRECTOR OF ATHLETIC TRAINING*

Before we got on the plane to Florida, we made an affirmation. Our special teams coach Greg McMahon, who I worked with at the Saints, talked about character and toughness. He said in his meeting that we were not coming back without a victory. I told the whole team, "I want every man before you get on this plane to take your right fist and punch it right in your jaw." It wasn't supposed to be a hard punch. But I wanted them to mentally commit that we were going to fight—and no matter what, we were not leaving Florida without a victory.

We had let Troy go. We had blocked out all of the noise. I had turned off Twitter. I didn't watch TV all week. I wasn't going to watch any sports on TV the rest of the season. I was totally immersed in our team.

We beat Florida, 17–16. The defense played well. We didn't give up any big plays. It was such a charged atmosphere. The Swamp was crazy that day. After the third quarter, Florida had come back from being down 17–3. Their fans probably were sure they were coming back to beat us.

Tom Petty, who is from Gainesville, had just passed away. Florida had started this tradition where going into the fourth quarter, the stadium plays his classic "I Won't Back Down." The whole crowd started singing. In my head, I was singing it too. Our guys really bowed up in the fourth quarter when it looked like the Gators might rally. We only allowed them one first down in the entire fourth quarter. It was hot as heck that day, but we found a way to win. When we got on the plane to fly home, there was a real sense of relief. You could feel it.

It was an unbelievable feeling we had from that win. We'd lost some games that we probably shouldn't have, and we were fighting our tails off. Hearing that crowd singing "I Won't Back Down," it was almost like they were talking to us. I talked to Coach the next day about it while we were doing the injury report. That was such a neat moment, how he was able to rally that team, and we had enough grit to pull that off. Who knows what would have happened if we lost that game?

—JACK MARUCCI, LSU DIRECTOR OF ATHLETIC TRAINING

Number ten Auburn was up next. Two weeks earlier they had whipped that Mississippi State team, 49–10. We had a crowd of almost 102,000 people for the hottest October kickoff in LSU history at ninety degrees. It was boiling. We were down 20–0 in the first half. Many of the fans had left the stadium. But I give our guys—and our staff—a lot of credit. Not one person on our team blinked.

We got after Auburn on defense in the second half. Devin White, our middle linebacker, was everywhere. He made fifteen tackles. Auburn only managed 64 yards in the second half after putting up almost 300 yards in the first half. They couldn't get anything done on third downs, going one for eight. We swarmed their quarterback, Jarrett Stidham, sacked him, harassed him. He ended up just nine of twenty-six for 165 yards.

We cut the lead to 23–14 going into the third quarter. D. J. Chark, who was the best player on the field that day, took a punt back 75 yards for a touchdown. Tiger Stadium was going crazy. We had heard there was a traffic jam trying to get out of there at halftime, and I guess there was a traffic jam from people trying to get back into the building. We went on to win, 27–23. It was the biggest comeback in Tiger Stadium in almost seventy years.

I give a lot of credit for that comeback to one of our analysts, Kevin Coyle, a long-time NFL coach who has been vital to our success at LSU. In the summer, our staff works on projects. Kevin came to me and said, "I've got something that you're really going to love." It was something he got from Paul Pasqualoni when I coached with him at Syracuse: a great sermon with some memorable points. He put it together, and I gave it to the team.

It really paid off. It was part of our Winning Edge program, where we really drill down into specific in-game scenarios to get our guys primed to be at their best when situations occur in the heat of the game, at crunch time. Kevin had talked to me about making sure your focus, no matter what is happening, no matter what the score, is all about winning the game. It sounds simple, but it's actually not that elementary. For the rest of the year we kept going back to the main inspiration of that talk: no matter what is happening in the heat of the game, you've got to find a way to be positive. Our guys know to speak only in terms of positive reinforcement.

We wanted to hear this kind of talk from them on the field:

- Here's what we're going to do to win the game. Stay together! Stay together! Hey, let that play go. Hey, they did this, so we're going to make this adjustment.
- Here's how we're going to attack that problem (and then drill down into it). We're going to bring the nickel off the edge, we're going to block the inside zone better—you're going to get your outside shoulder here.

It was an attitude that said, *Let's be a part of the solution.* They were to keep their minds focused on the details of the solutions. When they were down, I wanted them to speak in good football specifics—technique, alignment, effort. I didn't get them out of whack because a guy screwed up a play, wasting time on saying things like "I told you not to do this!" I've been around too many coaches who, in the heat of the battle, get caught up in speaking to the negative on the sideline. It only makes things worse.

Jimmy Johnson and Pete Carroll were very positive with the players during games. I saw it, but when I first became a head coach I didn't exercise it at Ole Miss. You've got to stay under control to do that. Too many times we, as coaches, get caught up in the emotions of the game. Football coaches often think that anything is okay in the heat of battle. Well, when you let the emotions get to you, you're really only hurting your team. It's like quicksand—the more you twist and fight it, the faster you go down. I've learned we have to be disciplined in how we communicate as coaches in-game. I do not allow that kind of chatter on the headset. My rule is, you only speak to your specific position. I'll tell 'em to calm down in a heartbeat.

In our comeback against Auburn that day, anyone could see their sideline going down, just like we could see the mental state of our sideline rising. I guarantee you that their sideline was chewing guys out as the game started to slip for them.

That win felt really good. The next week, though, we were playing Ole Miss. I was going back to Oxford. I knew people were going to try and make a big deal of my return there, but I wasn't getting caught up in any of that. This was just another SEC game to me. We challenged our team to play with a sense of urgency, and they did. We felt like we could run the ball on them, and we did. Our offensive line came out and played physical, and Derrius ran all over them for 276 yards. We won, 40–24—our third SEC win in a row before our bye week to get ready to go to number one in the country Alabama.

◀

Obviously, we knew that Alabama was a huge game for us. But I wanted to manage that excitement. I didn't want to make it bigger than life.

In years past, I think the Alabama game was made too big. It was all or nothing. And then after a loss, everything else would go downhill. The year before I took over, we lost to Alabama and followed that up with two more losses the next two games. The year before that, we lost to Alabama and then lost two of the next three after it.

In our team room, a big schedule board hangs on the wall. We drew the Alabama logo on the board, which is usually big script capital A in crimson. But we lowercased that *a* and put it in black. That's also how we put it on all of the pages of our scouting report. It was a subtle message, but I wanted to get that point across. I think it worked.

The Alabama Crimson Tide had beaten LSU six straight times, but our guys believed they could beat them in Tuscaloosa. We knew we could go toe-to-toe with them. That game we played loose and confident. We outgained them that night. We matched the physicality of their game. They carted seven of their players off the field. Not one of ours. We had a couple of great opportunities to hit big plays, with D. J. Chark open on a skinny post two or three times, but we just couldn't get him the ball. The final score was 24–10, but it felt much closer than that.

To beat Alabama, you have to match their physicality on both lines of scrimmage. We did. You also have to take advantage when the shots are there. We didn't. We had wide receivers running wide open, and couldn't get them the ball.

You have to have big guys to compete with that team. You can hope and wish and pray all you want, but you need the muscle too. Finally, our guys stood up to them and played with great technique. We were 320 pounds across the line. They had the mindset. Our big guys knew it was going to be a war, and we got underneath their pads on both sides of the line of scrimmage. I was proud of the team.

After the game, a reporter asked me if we had laid the groundwork to beat Alabama. I stopped him and said, "We comin'."

The press room got real quiet. I nodded my head so everybody knew I was serious. I didn't want to claim some moral victory. I wasn't joking around. We had matched Alabama's physicality. I could see it in our guys' eyes. The years before, we had a lot of trouble blocking them. But now I was fired up. It was very emotional after the game, and I was proud of the way our guys, especially up front, fought.

"We comin'. And we ain't backin' down."

I knew we weren't that far off. I guess some people thought I was trying to create a moment or a sound bite, but it was just a raw, honest expression of what I believed in my heart. It was how I saw things playing out at LSU, and in the college football world.

We ran through our next three SEC opponents, Arkansas, Tennessee, and Texas A&M, winning all three games by at least twenty points. After our loss to Troy, we ended up winning six of our next seven games. The defense kept improving. I felt like we had a lot of momentum. That dark cloud had lifted. We were headed to the Citrus Bowl for the second year in a row, this time to play Notre Dame to cap the season.

◀

To prepare for Notre Dame, I watched the Fighting Irish on film. I felt we were better than Notre Dame. The year before, we played Louisville in the Citrus Bowl and had one of our best games. And the players were disciplined that year. We imposed a curfew the first night, and all of the players were in, resting and preparing.

This time we went back to the same hotel, laid down the same curfew, but twenty-seven players missed curfew. It shocked me. The next day I had a team meeting, and I yelled at the top of my lungs. "I am so disappointed in you guys!" We were facing a lot of distractions at the Citrus Bowl. The team was wondering, *Is Canada gone?* I thought we had them in a good place mentally, but once we got down there, I knew their mindset was wrong.

That lack of focus carried over to the bowl game. A couple of false starts ruined drives. We missed a couple of short field goals. We led 17–14 with two minutes left in the game. We put the game in the defense's hands. We played a one-high coverage that left Donte Jackson, our fast, five-foot-nine corner, with a big receiver on him. Their six-foot-four receiver made a great one-handed catch along the sideline and went fifty-five yards for the touchdown. They won, 21–17.

I was disgusted.

We stayed over that night in Florida. The next morning, we got on the team plane. I told everyone, as soon as we landed, to go straight to the team meeting.

I was writing in my notebook the whole way home, getting angrier and angrier. I knew what was at stake.

As soon as we got back, I made sure they got the message. I told anyone who planned on coming back next year to go straight from the bus to the meeting. Some seniors came. Some didn't. Everybody on the staff showed up—except one coach who wasn't retained.

"Let me tell you something," I said. "This crap is over. I ain't putting up with any of this anymore. I am not going to disrespect anyone in here. We're gonna have a winning culture. You will go to class. You will be early. And this is the day that it is gonna start. If you're not going to do it, you're going to be in my office, and I'm holding you accountable. That individualism—the playing for yourself, all the distractions—is over. It's a shame we lost that game. We embarrassed everybody who ever wore the purple and gold. From now on, if you don't like it, leave right now. Please leave right now. And, that goes for any coach, any support staffer who isn't going to go all out for the LSU Tigers. If you're not in, you leave now."

There was silence. On an intensity scale of one to ten, I was at 9.9. I saw a couple of grimaces, but it didn't last long. I was going to call 'em out. I had had enough. I knew I had another year, and I wasn't going to let things slide. I thought to myself, *I've got one shot to get this fixed.* We'd gone 9–4. I understood the expectations. I had to find a way to be stern and hold them accountable and still treat them with respect.

After those twenty-seven kids missed curfew, I told them, "Listen—
y'all do not want Bebe to come out. He's big on this respect
thing." At the end of the day, Coach O was still trying to get a hold
of the team without destroying the team. He couldn't light into
them at that time after Mississippi State or Troy. Some of those
kids were about just getting to the NFL. There were a couple of
kids we had to get up out of there. I had to learn this playing at
Nebraska in the '90s. Just because that program won a whole
bunch of games, it's just not going to be like that every year. But
after that meeting, it was, "This is it. Enough is enough." I think
he looked them in their eyes, like a parent talking to a twenty-
year-old. He had their attention. They were thinking, *I'd better
not mess with this dude.* And, I'm telling you, from that time on,
it was a different program. After that, we had no curfew issues.

—*MICKEY JOSEPH, LSU ASSISTANT HEAD COACH*

It is definitely a tricky balance to manage a team. Each year,
each team is different. As we grew, they understood. We've got certain parameters, and you work inside those parameters. The minute
you step over the line, I will hold you accountable. And that is a
constant. I remembered something that Jimmy Johnson used to say
a lot at Miami: "I will coach the best players the hardest." I thought
that was important for the whole team to see. Sometimes, the juniors and the seniors start sliding. They start thinking about the
NFL. They've got people around them talking to them about
the NFL. We had to find a way to keep them with us.

At my previous schools, I had always been the intense discipli-
narian guy. Now, at LSU, I had gone too far in the other direction.
I went too soft, and it didn't work. I had to keep on fine-tuning my
approach to find the exact amount of tough love—the right combination of discipline and looseness.

Eventually we began recruiting the right guys, who understood this at the beginning. We talked to them and their parents about what we expected, and they got it early in the process. We also grew into a more cohesive staff of guys who knew what I wanted, and guys I could trust.

It took a while to figure out what standards were right for us and how to achieve them, but the key was deciding, deliberately, what excellence meant. Once we had a standard set, we could see our way toward reaching it.

◄13

THE LEAP
OF FAITH

◀

The first time I had ever heard of Joe Burrow was from my son, Cody. Ohio State had played its spring game the week before we played ours in 2018. Burrow threw a forty-two-yard touchdown pass on the final play of the Buckeyes' scrimmage. Cody watched it on TV and had been following Joe on social media. Cody called me—"Dad, this Joe Burrow is going to transfer from Ohio State. You've got to get him."

I went to Bill Busch, our safeties coach, who had spent a season at Ohio State in 2015 as a quality-control assistant—Joe's first season with the Buckeyes: "What do you think about us trying to get Joe Burrow here as a grad transfer?"

"If we get Joe Burrow, we're going to the College Football Playoff."

I said, "Let's go get him then!"

Joe got his release a few weeks later. Bill handled the transfer to LSU on our end because he knew the family. A lot of people knew Joe's dad, Jimmy Burrow. He was the defensive coordinator at Ohio. I figured there'd be a lot of competition to get Joe. His dad knew a lot of people I knew—even if I didn't realize that at the time. Jimmy had been in the Midwest for a long time, but we found out that he was actually from Mississippi but then he went to Nebraska to play for the Cornhuskers.

When Joe was coming out of high school in Ohio, he was a great basketball player and a very talented quarterback. He threw for a lot of yards and ran for a lot too. He was a first-team all-state point guard in basketball. His dad's alma mater, Nebraska, where Joe's older brothers Dan and Jamie played, didn't recruit him. He'd gone to Ohio State. He redshirted his first year, then spent two seasons as the backup to Buckeyes quarterback J. T. Barrett. Joe was a terrific student, made Academic All-Big Ten, and graduated from Ohio State in three years with a business degree. When the starting quarterback job came open, Urban Meyer opted to name Dwayne Haskins the starter.

We found out that, ultimately, it was going to be Joe's decision where he went next. Nebraska wasn't interested in him, we heard. Cincinnati was very interested in him. They had an in with him. Their head coach, Luke Fickell, used to be a Buckeyes assistant and knew him well. They had two other offensive coaches, Joker Phillips and Mike Hartline, who he was close to from their time together at Ohio State. Cincinnati was close to where he lived. We also found out that his girlfriend, who he'd met at Ohio State but had graduated, had moved back to Cincinnati where she was from. So if he transferred there, he could be close to her.

We heard that Cincinnati had promised Joe that he'd get the starting job. The day he walked on their campus, he was their starter. At LSU, we already had a three-quarterback battle for the starting job, with two of the guys having come in as top-ten QB recruits (Myles Brennan and Lowell Narcisse) and the third guy (Justin McMillan) being a favorite among his teammates. They were all talented guys with strong arms.

I tried recruiting Joe. He didn't want to talk much on the phone. But he agreed to come visit LSU. Joe had taken a one-day trip to Cincinnati before he came to Baton Rouge. I had a feeling he was planning on going to Cincinnati because it felt like home and he had that connection to Fickell. But we were going to take our shot with him.

I got into Baton Rouge before Joe landed there. I was the first one to meet Coach O. He was already pretty cool on my measuring scale to begin with. Then he went on my favorite podcast, *Pardon My Take*. That only made him cooler in my eyes. He told this amazing story about putting a live worm in his mouth—"I was a team captain in college and gave this motivational speech to the team. The story is about two men fishing in ice holes in Alaska. One guy was catching fish and the other wasn't. He said, 'Hey man, I'm using the same bait. Why am I not catching fish?' The other guy said, 'I have a secret. I keep the worms in my mouth to keep them warm, then I put them in. I'll do whatever it takes to feed my family.' I said, just like that fisherman doing whatever it takes to feed his family, I'll do whatever it takes to win. And then, I pulled a big, old worm out of my mouth." He was a dynamite storyteller—legendary. And he was excited to meet me. It was surreal. We were starting to build a relationship.

—DAN BURROW, JOE'S OLDER BROTHER

Foster Moreau, our tight end and one of the best people on our team, was Joe's host for the weekend. Joe came to eat with some of our coaches on Friday night at a Brazilian steakhouse. It went okay, but I could tell he didn't want to be recruited.

The next morning, we ate breakfast with his family. They were very nice. Then, we went to the office and sat around the long rectangular table in our staff room. It's me; Joe; his daddy, Jimmy; his brother, Dan, who'd come in from Houston; Steve, our passing game coordinator; Jerry Sullivan, a long-time NFL assistant; and Jorge Munoz, an offensive analyst who had been an offensive co-ordinator and a guy I leaned on a lot. We catered in lunch. Jorge did a good job of marrying what Joe did at Ohio State with some cut-ups of what we did at LSU, as well as some NFL techniques that we were going to implement into our offense. Jorge had pulled all of Joe's good plays from mop-up duty late in games and from Ohio

State's spring game. We wanted to take some of his plays that looked like our plays to help him think, *I was really good at that play*, so he'd see how it fit with what we wanted to do. We figured it would build a comfort zone, and a sense of trust and faith. We wanted him to be assured, *Hey, these guys understand me.*

When we started talking about Joe's plays, his reads, what he was seeing, attacking the coverages, that is when he really lit up. I have never heard another college player talk about football the way he did.

Our coaches started asking him questions like, "Why'd you like this? What did you see here? What was your footwork? What if the MIK linebacker blitzes? Do you like this play against an odd front or an even front?"

We really started learning about him. He was firing back answers. "The corner sloughed off. I knew I had to throw the slant . . . I saw he had outside leverage. I liked that matchup."

He didn't know beforehand that we were going to ask him about these plays or what we were going to talk to him about in that room. We just hit Play on the footage. And he already had all the answers and was able to explain what his mental process was. He did it in crystal-clear detail. Listening to him, what we were looking for really wasn't so much a matter of a right or wrong answer; it was more about his command of the process.

They did a lot of quarterback run and empty package at Ohio State. Some quarterback draws. They were running the power read, where the guard pulls up. Sometimes they'd kick the guard out. Sometimes they'd pull him. Joe was on top of all of it, explaining that it depended whether it was man or zone. I'd never heard that before. I just kept my mouth shut. As Joe kept explaining, you could feel the command he had over what he was talking about—and he was doing it in a room full of veteran coaches, many he'd never met before. That was when I knew he was the smartest guy in the room, smarter than everyone else in there. It wasn't hard to figure out. We probably were in there for three or four hours talking ball with him. I was sold.

What that meeting did for us was, one, we got to see they do have a good nucleus of players; and two, it convinced Joe in his mind that they were moving in a direction to open up the offense. People recruiting against LSU had been saying, "This is what LSU has done offensively. They don't seem to ever change. Is that what you really want?" Joe had been thinking, *Am I going to be under center 75 percent of the time?* He probably hadn't been under center since like the fifth or sixth grade.

—*JIMMY BURROW, JOE'S DAD*

That afternoon, I tried to bring Joe in the office and talk to him. He said to me, "Coach, I'm not into this recruiting stuff, okay?" I had never had a recruit talk to me like that. I said, "Joe, we've got a lot of great players here for you to throw the ball to. We just don't have a quarterback. You're going to be surrounded by great players." He said, "I know that, Coach."

When you get a recruit on campus, you're always looking for little private moments when you can get a better read on him— when you feel like you can make a connection. I knew he was not going to be on campus much longer. I felt like I was behind the eight ball. He would not let me squeeze him at all.

I didn't really think Joe would ever open up to Coach O while we were down there. That's just not Joe. He's pretty guarded. Maybe some of that comes from sitting there in the stands as a kid, listening to people badmouth your dad and your team. He went to his first game when he was four days old, when his dad was coaching the Iowa Barnstormers in the Arena League. Over the years, listening to some of that negative stuff, you're going to develop a thick skin. I know there were a lot of times I thought, *I wish my son wasn't sitting on my lap hearing some of these things.*

—*ROBIN BURROW, JOE'S MOM*

I liked Joe a lot. We were probably in my office less than ten minutes for our final conversation before he and his family left town. The more he tried to dodge all my recruiting tactics, the more I liked him. Knowing Joe now, I realize that was just him. He doesn't let any of the side stuff get in his way. He had a laser focus unlike any that I'd ever seen before. There was an unbelievable maturity about him. You could tell he was completely immersed in football.

Joe told me he wanted crawfish for dinner, so I took him to Mike Anderson's, the best seafood restaurant in town. Mike Anderson was an All-American at LSU, and his restaurant was the place where everybody in town went. The problem was, they ran out of crawfish that night. So I called Sharon Lewis in our recruiting department to phone another place in town, and they sent over twenty pounds of crawfish. They brought it through the kitchen like they made it themselves.

Joe opened up a little bit at dinner. He was with his mother, brother, and dad. It was a more casual, more relaxed atmosphere. Before we left the restaurant, I knew I had to take my shot. My gut told me that I had better have a little one-on-one with Joe. We walked outside, just me and him.

"I can't promise you the starting quarterback job," I told him. "But, Joe, you're going to be my starting quarterback. I have watched you on tape. I listened to you today in that room. I have total confidence that you're going to be our starting quarterback.

"Look at me, Joe. I have got to win here. I am putting it all on the line. You're going to be our starting quarterback. But I can't guarantee you the job right off the bat. I gotta be loyal to my players and give them a chance. I know the talent on this team. You will be my starting quarterback, though, if you come in and do the things you're supposed to do. And if the head coach thinks you should be the starting quarterback, guess who is going to be the starting quarterback?"

He just said, "I got you, Coach."

That was about it. I looked him right in the eye and he shook my hand. I could see that he respected me.

The whole weekend, I had thought he was planning on going to Cincinnati. But after that little talk outside Mike Anderson's, I felt we still had a chance. That might have been the most important talk I have ever had with a recruit.

I knew he'd just been at Ohio State and busted his butt; he had done everything he could do to prove he should lead that team and earn that job, but he didn't get it.

I knew he was probably hesitant for that reason, and wondering if he could trust us not to pass him over again. He would have to take a leap of faith to come to LSU.

But I thought this guy was off the charts. I just knew he had it.

Joe went back to Ohio. I called Foster to try and find out what Joe was thinking. Joe had told Foster that he was 70 percent leaning toward LSU. Foster thought, *Wait. Really?* He told me, "I think we have a really good shot."

We called Joe that night but he didn't answer. Monday morning, I called his older brother Dan. I thought he was a key to Joe. Dan was an honest guy, gung ho. I knew I'd made a good connection with him that weekend. He was the one who broke the ice that

Saturday. I was pretty sure he believed that LSU was the best place for his brother.

"Hey Dan! What's Joe going to do?"

"Well, Coach, it's his decision."

"Hey Dan, f*** that. LSU or Cincinnati? Listen Dan, I want you to reach down there and check your package. If you got two, you need to give him a call and tell him LSU is the best place for him. Are you going to let him go to Cincinnati instead of LSU, Dan?"

"Well, it's going to be up to Joe."

"Danny, if you love your brother and want what's best for him—and I know you do—you got to call him and be firm with him."

"Yes sir."

"I know you love your brother. And, you know that the best decision is for him to go to LSU. You got to be strong and forceful in how you say it."

"Yes sir."

I think Coach O gives me too much credit, although I certainly never would have put together a Microsoft Word document and come with a consultative approach to try and help Joe make a good decision if Coach O hadn't motivated me. At least, it wouldn't have been as well thought out as it was. This is not how our brother dynamic works. Joe is a smart kid. He's been through a lot. He can make this decision for himself. I texted Joe—"I'd love to share my thoughts on this situation." He wrote back, "Yeah, man."

I texted, "Joe, you told me that you want to compete at the highest level and play for championships. If those things are, in fact, true, there is only one place where you can accomplish your goals." I'd also written, "If you stay in Ohio, you will never escape the Ohio State / Dwayne Haskins questions. They are coming every single week, no matter who you are playing. You're not going to hear about Ohio State or Dwayne in Baton Rouge. It could be very therapeutic to put some distance between you and that whole situation. . . . One thing I've learned over the last few years is that sometimes in order to grow and get better, sometimes we have to get UNCOMFORTABLE."

—*DAN BURROW, JOE'S BROTHER*

Three days later, Joe called me.

"Coach, I've decided. I'm going to come to LSU."

Man, I was so fired up.

"I'm going to come down there and bust my ass."

I said, "I know you will."

I don't know if that talk [with Dan] had a huge part in my decision, but I definitely knew that my family wanted me to go to LSU. I think LSU was the spot the whole time in the back of my mind. I didn't think about being willing to become uncomfortable at the time, but that's something that I've always lived my life by. That saying goes back to preparation and work ethic in the off-season. You have to push yourself to the most uncomfortable parts of your life, your body, and your mind to go places that other people aren't willing to go, and to do things that other people can't do.

—*JOE BURROW*

I knew getting Joe was a big deal for us, but I didn't know at the time that Joe Burrow was going to prove to be the biggest recruit LSU had ever landed.

◀

That whole year we emphasized locking down the state of Louisiana in recruiting. A strong crop of in-state players was coming out that year, and a bunch of must-gets. Ja'Marr Chase was a guy we loved, as well as Terrace Marshall—everybody wanted those two receivers. Dare Rosenthal was a huge lineman we thought could be a high draft pick in the NFL. We really liked Damone Clark, a big, fast linebacker, but we also reached on and misevaluated some local guys too. We got most of them, but looking back, I stretched too much to keep those Louisiana kids home. We took several guys I wasn't sure about, but I just didn't want to let them go to Texas or someplace far away. I learned a lesson. I'm not doing that anymore. If I don't think he's an elite player, an elite prospect, I can't take him. I can't do that to this university.

We were coming up on signing day, and we thought we were going to get the top cornerback on our board, Patrick Surtain from South Florida. But we found out late the night before that he was going to Alabama. The bottom line was his daddy wanted him to play for Nick Saban, and not me. I thought back on his visit to LSU. His dad had looked at me and said, "I want my son to play for championships." I said, "Good, we're going to do it here." His face just turned. You could tell he wasn't buying it.

After we found out that we weren't getting Surtain, we reached out to another cornerback, but he'd accepted an offer from Clemson by then. We were looking at another dual-threat quarterback from Alabama who ended up picking Texas A&M. Then, when Surtain announced his choice on national TV, he said he picked Alabama because "they win championships, and I want to be a part of that."

It felt like a big, black cloud was hanging over signing day. I think the recruiting sites ranked our class number fifteen. Some people mocked us because we gave a spot to a kicker from some school nobody had ever heard of. But we knew we really needed a kicker, and we had been looking for the best grad-transfer kicker out there. I trusted our special teams coordinator Greg McMahon to find one. The good thing about those NFL guys like Greg was they're true evaluators. They don't get caught up in the hype, about whether someone is "a five-star guy" or whatever.

Greg had heard from a young coach who kicked for me at USC, Joe Houston, about a kicker named Cole Tracy from a division-two school in Massachusetts, Assumption College, which had only about two thousand students. In his junior year, Cole had gone twenty-seven of twenty-nine on field goals and sixty-seven of sixty-seven on extra points, and he won the Fred Mitchell Award that went to the best kicker in the five classifications below the FBS level. I'd never seen Cole kick until we got him, but I believed in Greg.

We ended up with one unfilled scholarship spot left over. That was the spot we needed to have room for Joe Burrow. It worked out perfectly. I'd take Joe over Surtain any day of the week. We knew Joe and Cole were going to help us, but we didn't realize they would help as much as they did. I prided myself on being someone who believed greatly in my ability to evaluate people, regardless of what others may have thought. Sometimes that means you're out there on the limb by yourself and that's okay. I was convinced it was going to be worth it.

◀14

TRUSTING YOUR LEADERS

Every year, Tommy Moffitt, our strength coach, gives the team his conditioning test the first Tuesday in June after they come back from their summer break. He's been doing a version of it since his days at Tennessee when he coached Peyton Manning. It's not easy, especially in that Louisiana heat. They've got to do sixteen ninety-yard shuttles, going thirty up, thirty back, and then thirty up. They get a one-minute rest between each. Then, they get a five-minute break after the sixteenth shuttle. Receivers and backs have to do each in under fifteen seconds. Quarterbacks, tight ends, fullbacks, and linebackers have to do it in under seventeen. Linemen have to do it in under nineteen seconds. Then, they have to do sixteen 110-yard sprints. Same time limits. And, if they don't pass, they've got to keep on doing it every Friday until they pass it.

Joe Burrow arrived in 2018 a week earlier than he was supposed to be in Baton Rouge. While everyone else was still on their vacation, he was out there going through that workout with Coach Moffitt. He had told Tommy, "My first impression is going to be important. I don't want to be like another freshman or newcomer." He didn't want to look lost. He wanted to crush it.

I was there at 6:00 a.m. watching Joe compete at every rep and win every rep. I was glad to see it. I needed to let this happen. I knew a transition was going to take place for Burrow to take over the team. Really, it was a transformation.

When Joe first got to Baton Rouge, tight end Foster Moreau would go catch passes with him. All the other guys went with the other three quarterbacks. Maybe it was out of favoritism; maybe just out of familiarity. The team, at that point, thought that Justin McMillan was going to be our quarterback.

We graded everything in camp—every drill, every seven-on-seven rep, all of the one-on-ones, everything from the team scrimmages. We kept all their scores in a book. I figured I was going to need it.

A couple of weeks after our first scrimmage of camp, offensive coordinator Steve Ensminger told all four quarterbacks about where they stood on the grades. We tried to give everybody equal reps. That's a lot of quarterbacks to try and get reps for with the season coming up. Joe and Myles Brennan were the top two guys based on the grades, followed by Justin and Lowell Narcisse.

Shortly after Steve told them, Lowell came to my office to tell me he wanted to transfer. I didn't want him to leave, but thanked him for telling me. When we went out to practice, Justin McMillan was not there. He had left the team without telling me.

That night, Justin called Coach Ensminger and said he wanted to come back. Steve told him that he had to ask me. At that point, Justin quitting had become a big distraction to the rest of the team. I said, "You did it the wrong way. You quit the team without telling me. I can't let you back on the team right now."

Justin talked to the team that night. The next day, our leadership committee said they wanted to hear from me, asking why I didn't let Justin back. The players were pissed and needed to hear from me.

The team didn't know exactly what had happened. Just that Justin was gone. A lot of rumors were swirling. At our leadership committee meeting, they went around the table and each guy voiced his opinion. It got heated, but it was healthy. They didn't know that Justin hadn't come to tell me initially that he was leaving. He had just left. I explained that we couldn't keep repping four quarterbacks. I said, "Guys, here are the grades." I had printed out the results to show them.

Some of the players said the grades were wrong.

"Do you think I'd actually do something to harm the team?" I asked them. "My ass is on the line too. I recruited every one of y'all. Do you think I wouldn't play the best quarterback here? Y'all trust me?"

They wanted Justin McMillan to be the starter. Justin is talented. He could make plays—he has a strong arm, could throw on the run—but he was very inconsistent.

They didn't have to tell me what I wanted to hear. They knew that. Just like a family, they were vocal. A lot of our strongest leaders on the team, especially guys on the defense—Rashard Lawrence, K'Lavon Chaisson, Devin White, and Michael Divinity—said that if Joe was the best quarterback, they were going to get behind Joe.

"Coach, we're behind you."

"So what are we going to do?" I asked them.

"Let us have a team meeting, a players-only meeting," they said. "Coach, we're going to talk to the team. We got the right story. We know what happened. We trust you."

I said, "Good—tell them the truth."

The coaches stayed outside in the hall. Most coaches were okay with it. Some of them were unsure how it was going to play out and what was going on in there.

Their meeting lasted about forty-five minutes.

Hearing that Joe was right now the number one guy and then Myles was number two caught the team off guard. Joe had brought a completely different style to the room. At first, I don't think they knew what to make of him. The guys heard it as, "We're going with a guy that we know the least about." But guys stood up for Joe. Devin stood up for Joe. Devin said, "If this is what we've got, we're riding with him 100 percent."

> Greedy Williams stood up for Joe. Mike Divinity was a big voice
> in the locker room and stood up for Joe. Also, we knew that
> defensively, we were going to be good. And, we had been on
> the ride for so long, we didn't think it was out of the norm.

—FOSTER MOREAU

I trusted those guys were going to do what they said they were going to do in there, and I never looked back. To this day, I still don't know much of what was said in there. I never asked. That was my team, and I trusted them. The black cloud seemed to lift afterward. It was tense in there, but they achieved some much-needed clarity.

> I just sat in the meeting and listened for a while. I knew that a lot
> of people on the team were rooting for Justin. I think Justin was
> kind of in the same position that I was at Ohio State. I know a lot
> of people at Ohio State wouldn't have liked someone transferring
> in to take my job if that had happened to me. So I addressed that,
> and told them that whether I'm the starter or not, whoever is the
> starter, we've got to rally behind that guy because we have to win
> games. I don't know how much my words resonated with anybody,
> but I think after that meeting, we were a lot closer as a team.

—JOE BURROW

I've got to commend the team for how they addressed that issue. That was a turning point in our program.

From then on, Joe Burrow started to gradually win over that team. It was a tight race for the job. One day, Joe was the best guy. Another day, Myles was. Another day, Justin had been. That first training camp, to be honest, Joe's arm wasn't that strong. I think his arm got tired because he had been throwing so much over the summer. Joe hadn't played football in three years, and he was working hard. He didn't have a lot of zip on his throws, but we knew he had all the intangibles. Somehow, some way, his arm strength developed here, and that's a credit to Steve Ensminger, Tommy Moffitt, and Jack Marucci, our trainer, and especially to Joe.

I knew there was some turbulence around the team. We had three players-only meetings during camp. That is a lot. But I didn't view it as a bad thing. We needed it. I wanted my guys to feel invested in our program. I trusted the leadership we had in that locker room. We had more vocal leaders than the previous season, and the team had become closer. Their vibe said, "This is our team now. Let's go!"

◀

We had been picked by the SEC media to finish fifth in our division. We didn't have a proven running back. We had an inexperienced group of receivers, a quarterback who hadn't played in the past three years, and an offensive line that didn't have much depth. I didn't think we were overly talented, but I believed we would be coached well and we were going to play hard—and that was going to win a lot of games.

Despite all the outside noise, I was optimistic about where we were headed. I hired James Cregg, who I had worked with at Tennessee and USC, to be our offensive line coach. He'd come from the NFL. I thought he was a tireless worker and outstanding coach. I loved our staff. I finally felt like we were all pulling in the same direction. In 2016, when I took over, most of our staff was pulling in the same direction, but not all. In 2017, we had more distractions on the staff. But in 2018, I felt we were a more cohesive unit. I moved Steve Ensminger back to offensive coordinator—he was my guy and I trusted him. Steve is a great coach and a great Tiger. He's very knowledgeable. People don't give him enough credit. The guy works his butt off. He's been the glue holding things together for me since I took over.

I'd always wanted to go to the spread offense from the time I was at Ole Miss. When I took over at LSU, we really didn't have the personnel for it. In 2016, we had two great running backs with Derrius and Leonard Fournette. We had a lot of twelve personnel with one back and two tight ends. It was from under center and a lot of play-action passing. In 2018, I wanted to go to four-wide receiver sets but we really couldn't. Steve said we just didn't have the guys to do it. I could say I wanted to go to the spread, but it's not like I could flip our roster overnight.

I had faith in Joe Burrow. I knew his DNA. I didn't panic, but I needed to be fair with the quarterback battle. Let the best man win. I'm all about the competition, and I believed it was going to make us better. Eventually, they all became friends. Joe kept on winning and he just worked his way into the team. It was wonderful the way he did it.

During fall camp, the defense was dominating. Devin White was chirping the whole time. "Yeah, that play don't work!" The third time he said something, all of a sudden, Joe yelled back, "Hey Devin, shut up. Or else I'm going to come over there and beat the f*** out of you!"

Joe hadn't even won the job yet. But that's what earned his respect. Joe's not a rah-rah guy. He's not going to give a speech. I think that was Joe being Joe, a tough northern kid; an Ohio guy. He doesn't take s***. He has so much inner strength. I think that's what Devin White wanted. He was wanting someone to respond and challenge him. Our team rallied around it, and

I think it had a snowball effect. "Hey, man this is our guy." The other quarterbacks for two or three years didn't say anything. A week later, Joe had a great scrimmage. We found out that was Joe. When bad things happen to him, he plays better because of it. Most kids tank it. He just has that "it" factor.

—JORGE MUNOZ, FORMER LSU OFFENSIVE ANALYST

It was clear that we had found a good leader, and we were ready to invest in him.

The defense was kicking our butts. I think that had kind of been that way for a long time. They like to talk s*** and all that stuff. There weren't a lot of people talking back on offense. I just got tired of it one day and started talking back. And then, there wasn't as much talk then from the defense. I just don't think they'd ever heard the quarterback do that before. I can't speak for them, but I know that after that, we were a little closer as a team. After that, I think I got some more people on my side.

—JOE BURROW

◀15

"HE KNOWS MY NAME NOW"

We opened the 2018 season against number eight Miami in Texas at AT&T Stadium, where the Dallas Cowboys play. We named Joe as our starting quarterback. We were barely ranked at number twenty-five. The game was on a Sunday night, so everyone in the country was watching because we were really the only game on. It was a heck of a challenge for us. I knew we were going to play well. Our backs were against the wall again. I thought every game that year was going to be a challenge.

It was a fun trip to Texas. Our guys went to Jerry Jones's stadium and got to look up at the big Jumbotron. We were underdogs coming into the game. Miami had a good defense.

On our third series, we had a second-and-fifteen. Joe noticed Miami's safety creep down into the box like he was going to blitz off the right side. Joe audibled to a run to the right. Our running back Nick Brossette hit the hole for a fifty-yard touchdown, giving us a 10–3 lead.

Joe really made that play. That was the thing that broke the game open to me. We finally made a play, and he did it with his mind. That showed everybody that he could put us in the right position and think fast on his feet. Then, on our next drive, we had a fourth-and-one at the Miami forty-nine-yard line. I told them we're going for it.

We called an off-tackle run to the right side, but their safety had moved up near the line, right where our play was supposed to go. Joe spotted it and checked out of the play and into a run to the left side. Nick ran for a short gain and picked up the first down. Seven plays later, we scored another touchdown to go up 17–3. That was such a big play in the game, and a big swing. That set a tone: it was like me saying, "I trust you guys and I trust our quarterback."

We scored thirty unanswered points to go up 33–3 and won 33–17. Cole, our new kicker, made all four of his field goal tries, including a fifty-four-yarder that tied a school record. It was a great night.

If you're going to talk about the impact a quarterback makes for a team, you usually talk about touchdown passes—but the two biggest plays of the game were ones where Joe didn't throw the ball. They were plays he made with his mind. I think that got the fans fired up. That gave the players more confidence. We didn't have that before. We hadn't had a guy like that since I'd been there.

To be considered a great quarterback at LSU, you've got to win the big games. And that was a big game. The only negative was we lost our best pass rusher, K'Lavon Chaisson, for the season to a knee injury during the game. We were really going to miss him. But I loved what I saw from our new quarterback and the impact he was making on our team. I knew he was going to build off that game.

When I got there, I was still kinda leery, even going into fall camp. I didn't really know if I was going to be the starter or not. Then, I got named the starter and never really looked back. But even throughout that first year, my mindset going into the next year, was that I still had to win the job. I had talked about it with people and they told me it wasn't true, but that's how your mind starts working after you don't play for three years and feel like you deserved to play. So, it was really difficult to trust at the beginning.

—*JOE BURROW*

◀

Six days later, we shut out Southeastern Louisiana to go to 2–0 before we had to visit number seven Auburn. We knew they'd be ready for us because we'd rallied from being down 20–0 a year earlier. They'd already won a big game in their opener, beating number six Washington. They had a thirteen-game home winning streak. We were a double-digit underdog against Auburn. It was a really hot day. Our guys competed their butts off.

They had the best defensive line in the SEC. We had a really inexperienced offensive line, and things looked even worse after our left guard, Garrett Brumfield, who was the vocal leader of our line, was knocked out of the game with a shoulder injury. We had to turn to a true freshman, Chasen Hines, a smart kid with nimble feet who we had converted from defensive line in camp. It was next man up, and for a true freshman, Chasen played an excellent game, especially against the guys he was facing on the road in an environment like that. Chasen never got caught up in the moment. We had a sophomore, Austin Deculus, starting at right tackle for Adrian Magee, who had gotten hurt in the Miami game. Austin played well too.

We relied on four guys we'd recruited and signed in the previous two classes, and they all came through. I knew that would bode well for the future. We had gotten bigger, tougher, and more athletic in the trenches through recruiting, and we did that by not chasing those star rankings. We did it by going after toughness and character, and trusting our own evaluations.

Auburn's defensive line didn't get any sacks all day, and their defense only got one. We outgained them and had more than a ten-minute edge in time of possession. They had us down 21–10, but our guys fought back again. Joe took some shots downfield. He hit a seventy-one-yard touchdown pass to Derrick Dillion to close the margin to 21–19. We got the ball back, and Joe led us downfield again to give us a chance. Cole, our new kicker, split the uprights perfectly from forty-two yards out on the game's final play. Hallelujah! I give Greg McMahon all the credit for finding Cole.

Cole would take his lunch breaks to sit down in Tiger Stadium and visualize his kicks. When we signed him, I thought he was going to be good. I didn't realize he would be as great as he was. If it's on the line, I want him out there. I don't think I'd ever had a kicker like that. At that point, I didn't care what other people were saying about my team because I knew that when you've got heart, a smart quarterback, a really good defense, and a really good kicker, you always got a chance.

A month later, we had moved up to number five in the country. We played Florida in the Swamp. Tim Tebow was getting inducted into their ring of honor. The crowd got to us. We did not play well. We didn't protect well. They sacked Joe five times and hurried him eight more times. He had come into the game without having thrown a pick all season, but he threw two in the game, including a pick-six.

Defensively, we were out of sync. We got beat on both lines of scrimmage. Dan Mullen, who had given us problems when he was the head coach at Mississippi State, got us again. It was a little bit different—not the same plays we had issues with in Starkville—but we still couldn't stop it. We got outcoached that day. We lost, 27–19.

We didn't have much time to lick our wounds, though. Number two Georgia was coming to Tiger Stadium the next week. We were a touchdown underdog in our own building.

I woke up that morning in Baton Rouge feeling really good, like we were going to beat them. I could just feel it. Our guys were ready to go. The place was electric.

We had a couple of big moments in that game when our guys

really answered the bell. The first one was when they tried a fake field goal early on. Grant Delpit made one of the smartest and most athletic plays I have ever seen. He was rushing off the left side. He felt the tight end release. He planted his foot and went and tackled the kicker and caused a fumble. That was a huge momentum play for us. Then, they started gashing us on their second series with runs of twelve, eighteen, and seventeen yards, shoving the ball right down our throats, running inside zone, with the combination block on the nose tackle. Their big tailback, Elijah Holyfield, ran right over my safety and was hitting that hole like a friggin' freight train. I told Dave Aranda we had to make an adjustment.

We were playing a shade defensively. I told Dave to go to a zero. That meant moving our 330-pound nose tackle, Ed Alexander, from playing as a one-technique shaded over one of the shoulders of the center to head up on their center. They'd run for sixty-nine yards on that second series. After we made that change, Georgia managed just forty-four rushing yards on nineteen carries the rest of the day. Ed had the best game of his college career.

The night before the game, I said, "Rougarou, stand up!" (That was Ed's nickname.)

"Their center don't even know your name. He thinks he's gonna whip your ass."

The whole room went quiet. He was staring at me. I thought Georgia's center was the best I'd seen in a few years at his position. On film, he was annihilating people. I was trying to motivate Ed in front of the whole team. I knew he wouldn't take that the wrong way. We had a good enough relationship that I thought I knew how he'd respond to that.

After the game, we were all celebrating in the locker room, when Ed said, "Coach, I got something to say."

He'd never said anything like that. He said, "He knows my name now! He knows my name now!" The team went nuts. It was beautiful. It could have been in a movie.

That was a big day for our offense too. We put up almost five hundred yards on them and outrushed them 275–113. We beat Georgia, 36–16.

We had stayed aggressive and taken advantage in crucial situations, going four-for-four on fourth downs. We surprised them one time, going for it from our thirty-seven yard line, and Joe ran for the first down. We kept drives alive. Joe had a big day with his arm and his legs, burning them. That was his coming-out party. If you're an LSU quarterback and you beat the number two team in the country, people start having confidence in you.

The next week, we beat Mississippi State, 19–3. We rose up to number three in the polls just in time for number one Alabama to come to Baton Rouge.

Our crowd was primed for that night. We weren't. We couldn't move the ball. We couldn't do anything. We were hanging in there on defense, but eventually, the defense broke.

We were max protecting, and they were still whipping us up front. Joe got sacked five times. Quinnen Williams, their star defensive tackle, singlehandedly destroyed us. We tried everything with him. We slid the line to him. We tried to double-team him. Lloyd Cushenberry and Damien Lewis, our two best offensive linemen, couldn't handle him. He had ten tackles, three and a half TFLs, and two and a half sacks. It was amazing how he dominated that game. We lost, 29–0. It was very disappointing. That was the eighth time in a row Alabama had beaten LSU.

The next morning, I went to Steve Ensminger and said we had to go to more of the spread. He said, "Coach, I agree with you." That's when we started transitioning them.

A lot of what we'd been doing that season was old NFL stuff that we had implemented from our passing game coordinator, Jerry

Sullivan. Against Alabama that day, we had been exposed. Our offensive tackles were getting their butts whipped and we had been going to full seven-man slide protections to try and help them out. We were only sending three guys out in the route, on deep routes. They were dropping seven guys back into coverage and rushing four and still swarming Joe.

We had no empty packages. There weren't any look-overs and see-what-they're-in-and-go calls. The ball wasn't coming out quick enough. We hadn't really bought into the run-pass options yet. We were still just lining up in a formation and running a play. Those days are over in college football. I knew we had to hire somebody to teach us the spread.

Our whole system had to change to get us to where we wanted to go.

◀

What happens in seven-man protection is when teams are playing in man-to-man, our tight end and running back are both blocking. The guys that are man-to-man on them, end up blitzing because they see that they're blocking and they don't have to cover them. So, when we were in seven-man protection, half the time I actually had less time to throw the ball than if I were in five- or six-man protection. I vented to Munoz about that a lot. He was my voice in the room for about a year and a half until I felt comfortable speaking up about stuff, when I was playing well enough in spring ball and fall camp to talk about it.

—*JOE BURROW*

As painful as that Alabama game was, we still had a chance to win ten games, which I knew was a big step for our program. We were 9–2 when we played Texas A&M on the road.

We didn't play well as a team. They played their best game. We were down 17–7 late in the first half. Joe threw a touchdown pass late in the fourth quarter to give us a 31–24 lead. We picked off a pass in the final minute. Our guys celebrated. I got doused with Powerade.

The officials reviewed the play and determined that their quarterback, who had fumbled the snap, actually had his knee touch the ground, blowing the play dead before he threw the pass. Then, A&M had the ball at our forty-one-yard line with ten seconds left. They completed a pass inside our twenty. The clock stopped with three seconds left. They had no timeouts remaining. The refs spotted the ball. The clock started. They didn't get the snap off in time.

0:00.

The refs reviewed it again and put one second back on the clock. A&M hit a touchdown pass. I don't think they should have put that second back on the clock. That's something I'm always going to disagree with, but we still had a chance to win.

Our guys fought hard. You never want to blame the refs for a loss. We had some stupid penalties; we dropped a punt. Some of our best players didn't make the plays they should have made—plays they usually make. We didn't have a good enough defensive game plan. We lost, 74–72 in seven overtimes.

Joe displayed incredible toughness and resolve that night. He had to have two IVs in his body back in the locker room. After the game, our busses had to be held back waiting for him.

Before the Texas A&M game, I think they were scared to run me all year because we just had me and Myles. And Myles wasn't quite what he became [in 2019]. Coach O called me in there, "Hey, we're gonna run the s*** out of you this game. We're gonna put the ball in your hands. Go win us the game." I said, "Hell, yeah! Let's do it."

> I ran the ball thirty times that game. I ran for a hundred yards. We ended up losing, but we played well on offense. Texas A&M was the real turning point, I think, when people started to realize I could do it and that our best bet to win a lot of football games was to put the ball in my hands forty to fifty times a game. After Alabama, we played Arkansas the next week, and we played like crap that game too. Then, after that, we had started to do more four-wide [receiver sets]. It started against Rice the week after. We had our first three-hundred-yard game passing. Against Texas A&M, we were in four-wide, five-wide. That's when the transformation started.
>
> —*JOE BURROW*

Even though we didn't beat A&M in the seven-overtime game, we got invited to the Fiesta Bowl to play number seven University of Central Florida. It was the first time LSU had been in a New Year's Six bowl, and we had the chance to have a ten-win season. We knew that was going to be a huge accomplishment for the team.

People were still questioning my hire. I knew that. But I was looking at the improvement of the program, blocking out the noise. I felt if we could win ten games, it would give us a big jump in recruiting and a lot of momentum for the next year.

UCF was riding a twenty-five-game winning streak. We felt they had an edge to them—that they played with a big chip on their shoulders. They had a lot of speed, especially on offense. I thought their defense was okay, but not great. But I was nervous about stopping their offense.

We went into the game down seven starters on defense because of injuries, guys sitting out the bowl to get ready for the NFL draft, and because of athletic department suspensions. And then we faced more adversity in the game, with two more defensive backs getting ejected in the first half, including our best defensive back, Grant

Delpit, who got kicked out for a targeting call. Other guys stepped up, though. Jontre Kirklin and Mannie Netherly came over from offense to play defense in the game.

The most adverse situation occurred midway through the first quarter. We were down 7–3 and driving deep into their territory. Joe threw an out route to their sideline. Our receiver slipped down. Their defensive back picked it and took off up the sideline. Then Joe got blindsided by their defensive lineman and they went ninety-three yards for a pick-six to take a 14–3 lead. Joe was down, and it didn't look good. Their team was whooping it up. Their fans were going crazy.

I was arguing with the officials for a targeting call. It was cheap—a really dirty play. I had to challenge it. Their player spit on Joe after the play. It got personal then. I saw Joe walk off the field slowly to our sideline. It looked like he had blood under his chin.

"Get Myles ready!" I yelled for Myles Brennan, our backup quarterback, to loosen up to take over for Joe.

"F*** that!" I heard Joe yell back. Right then, I knew he wasn't coming out of the game after that.

I thought, *Okay, here we go.* That moment turned that game, and not in the direction that UCF probably thought.

From there, Joe took it to another level. I saw something different in that kid. He was the most ultimate competitor I'd ever been around. He doesn't get rattled. When adversity hits, he actually gets better.

Joe came right back into the game and led us on touchdown drives our next three series, throwing touchdown passes to cap each of them. We went up, 24–14.

We hadn't installed anything too different scheme-wise late in the season, but we had gone to more four-receiver sets and the ball was coming out faster. We knew that Joe was more comfortable with that.

Right before halftime, UCF connected on a long pass play to

narrow it to 24–21. I felt when they threw that long ball on us, our heads were down. It took every ounce of energy I had at halftime to get that team going again.

We didn't have much depth left, but we had our team leaders: Joe and Rashard Lawrence took over on each side of the ball. We beat UCF, 40–32, to get our tenth win, ending their twenty-five-game winning streak. We won a New Year's Six bowl. I knew it didn't meet all of LSU's expectations, but I felt that we were on our way.

◄

That season taught the team a good lesson about blocking out the noise, with everything we had to fight through. We could see the culture of our program coming together. As opposed to the previous year, when I had to have that come-to-Jesus meeting with them immediately after the bowl loss as soon as we flew back in town.

We had a totally different mindset. We went out there and had fun. Everybody was in on time for curfew. We enjoyed being with our teammates. It was the first time a lot of our guys had seen a cactus or a mountain. And getting to ten wins was a tremendous accomplishment for our team.

After that Alabama game, as we started to transition our offense with more four-receiver sets and getting the ball out faster, Joe finished the year throwing ten touchdowns and just one interception and completed 67 percent of his passes, which was up from 53 percent and six touchdowns and four interceptions before that. We felt we had found something that really fit him—and us—much better. We just had to keep expanding on it offensively, and I had a plan for that. I knew we were close to where we needed to get. Plenty of people had discounted our players, but they had rallied. They knew our names now.

◀16

FIRE IN THE HOLE

Midway through the 2018 season, Jerry Sullivan, our seventy-four-year-old passing game coordinator, told me he was planning on retiring. I knew exactly who I wanted to hire as his replacement.

The previous summer, I had asked Greg McMahon, our special teams coordinator, to reach out to his old colleagues with the Saints. I wanted our staff to speak with them about New Orleans' red zone, empty, and two-minute packages. I said, "While you're at it, ask if they've got anybody on their staff who could come in and talk about RPOs."

The Saints weren't a big RPO—run-pass option—team, but Pete Carmichael, their offensive coordinator, said he had just the guy. I had never heard of Joe Brady till he came with Pete to Baton Rouge that day. Joe was a twenty-eight-year-old offensive assistant with New Orleans. He'd come from Penn State, where they crushed people with their RPO game.

When Joe Brady came with Pete to Baton Rouge, he brought with him some old Penn State film, Chiefs and Eagles film, and some notes about what he'd noticed from all his time with the Saints breaking down film. Joe was a meticulous notetaker. He would tag stuff that caught his eye and had built a lot of files of things that he liked. Every week, Joe Brady sat with Saints head coach Sean Payton for about an hour when he studied the NFL's touchdown tape of every score in the league from the previous weekend. Sean was always looking to see what they could adopt. I think that really helped shape Joe's thinking on offensive football. Plus, he got to be around Drew Brees, and that was invaluable for a young coach.

I was in and out of the room for both Pete and Joe's presentations to our staff that day because I was meeting with some of the Saints personnel people. But our coaches raved about Joe. He seemed like the perfect guy to allow us to completely go to the spread and build off of what Steve was doing. Until then, it felt like we had one foot in and one foot out in terms of our commitment to the spread. I wanted to go in all the way.

> When we were driving back to New Orleans that afternoon, I told Joe, "I think you just got a job." He started to laugh it off. I said, "I guarantee you in the next couple of years, Coach Orgeron is going to call you for a job."

—PETE CARMICHAEL, SAINTS OFFENSIVE COORDINATOR

Everybody Greg McMahon and I knew in the Saints organization was high on Joe Brady. I wanted somebody who was young and innovative, and that was him. Another one of our assistant coaches, John DeCoster, who had played high school football with Brady in South Florida, also had great things to say about him. The only other candidate I considered for the job was John Morton, who had been an assistant at USC and in the NFL, including a couple of seasons with the Saints. I knew Brady didn't have a long résumé and hadn't been a full-time position coach, but in my gut, I felt like he was the guy.

Brady's mindset was aggressive. He was all about dictating to the defense: "Okay, so you have these freak defensive linemen, why are we asking our guys to sit back and try to block them for seven seconds? Let's get all our guys out in their routes and attack them, where they've got to try and cover everybody."

I met with him again and liked his presentation and the way he carried himself. I told Sean Payton I wouldn't hire him until after the Saints' season was over. They lost in the NFC Championship Game. We hired Joe Brady a few days later.

Right after the news broke about who we hired, I got a call from one of our rivals in the SEC West, Joe Moorhead, the head coach at Mississippi State, who Brady had learned under at Penn State.

"You don't need to hear it from me," he said, "but you just got a great one."

◀

When Joe Brady got to LSU, things changed fast. He ripped out our old offense and brought in something new and fresh. I would get to work every morning at 6:00 a.m., and by then, the offensive guys were already meeting. You could just feel their enthusiasm about the changes Joe was bringing. It was a night-and-day difference from anything LSU had done before on offense. He had three-level looks and triangle reads for the quarterback: "If they do this, we're going to do that." He always had an answer. I felt we had a young Sean Payton or another Sean McVay. I knew Joe was good, but I honestly didn't know he was going to be as great as he was. I watched our offense change right in front of my eyes. He brought everybody on our staff and in our program so much confidence. They couldn't wait to come to practice. The players were walking around with a bounce in their step. Watching Joe operate was really something to see.

Joe Brady tied together our system with the hurry-up and the one-word calls. It was easy. It was quick—*Bam! Bam! Bam!* People were wide open in this offense. It was so impressive. He and Steve meshed so well. Steve busted his ass to learn this system. He bought in completely. Steve is like John Wayne: when he agrees on something, he means it. Deep down, I knew he was angry that we didn't score any points against Alabama the previous year. He wanted a little revenge.

Joe would handle red zone and third downs. Steve actually made about 80 percent of the calls. Joe brought the RPOs that he learned from Moorhead at Penn State and took the empty and quick stuff from the Saints. What Joe Brady brought fit perfectly with what Joe Burrow was most comfortable doing, when it came to being in the shotgun, going empty (formation), and putting five guys out there. That's what Joe Burrow had wanted, and that's what we needed.

Because of how well we'd recruited with the receivers, we had Justin Jefferson, Ja'Marr Chase, and Terrace Marshall, and the best all-around running back since I'd been at LSU in Clyde Edwards-Helaire. Everything was coming together at just the right moment.

Coach Joe brought in great things that Coach E adopted and made his own. We built it all together. They asked for my input a lot. I think they were just looking for the best way to put me in comfortable situations to maximize my talents and maximize the talents of our players. And, as people saw, we had very, very talented players, so we wanted to create as much space as possible for those guys to go to work.

—JOE BURROW

We had a lot of positive energy going into the 2019 season.

◀

In January, not long after the 2018 season ended, I started sitting down in the staff room at 6:00 a.m. to study our offensive and defensive line play. I had six other staffers in there with me. We'd watch practice film, drill tapes, scrimmages, and our old game film.

I really wanted us to get deep into the details and technique of line play. We had put together a great staff with a lot of experience.

It was myself; our offensive line coach, James Cregg; offensive analyst Mark Hutson, a former two-time All-American guard at Oklahoma who in 2018 was the assistant O-line coach for the Cleveland Browns; our defensive line coach, Dennis Johnson; graduate assistant coach Christian LaCouture, who played for us and had just retired after a stint in the NFL; Jorge Munoz, a former FBS offensive coordinator; and Charlie Baglio, who works in external affairs for our program and has been on the LSU football coaching staff since 2002 when Nick Saban hired him to help run his recruiting office.

We'd analyze each rep multiple times from two different camera angles, sometimes going frame by frame. I knew we could all learn from each other, and it was a great way to emphasize development and those critical little details. It also gave me better insight into our players and our coaches. If you have two sets of eyes on something, you can see it two different ways. We called it the O-line/D-line Appreciation Hour, although it usually only lasted about fifty minutes. The offensive and defensive staffs liked to have their own meetings at 7:00 a.m. By spring football, our O-line/D-line Appreciation Hour had doubled in size to twice as many coaches sitting around the table with us. It was invaluable, because those "little" details—like where a guy's hand is placed, how his toe is turned, where his eyes are—can be the difference between a touchdown or a tackle for loss.

I knew going into 2019, our offensive line play was a question mark. We ranked number thirteen in the SEC in sacks allowed, but we also had to get a lot better on the defensive line too. We had finished number seven in the SEC in run defense, and Florida and Alabama both ran through us in two of our losses. I knew if we locked in, we could fix both of those things.

◀

Our offense got after our defense in the spring like I'd never seen before. The ball was coming out so much faster. Joe Burrow was in complete control. The receivers were making plays all over the field. Receiver Ja'Marr Chase looked like he was going to be an All-American. We had our weapons and I knew we were going against some really good players every day at practice. I also knew that ratcheting up the level of competition between our offense and the defense was going to make us closer as a team, and better.

> My first year really felt like the offense was a team and the defense was a team. We weren't the LSU Tigers. It was just offense and defense. That really changed the next off-season. We became super close as a team, on and off the field. That spring, practices were super competitive. We were getting in fights. We were competing our tails off. I think that probably helped bring us closer. Spring ball was very intense. That gained some respect on both sides, and I think that carried over into the locker room.
>
> —*JOE BURROW*

I freakin' loved seeing how our offense had started standing up to the defense. The offense suddenly had an edge to it. In our last practice before the spring game, the offense had the ball around the twenty-five-yard line, going in. I was standing right behind Joe Burrow. Our defense blitzed. JaCoby Stevens, our big safety, came free. He jumped up to bat the ball down. He landed on Joe. It wasn't a vicious play, but because of JaCoby's size and strength, Joe went down. There was a little scuffle. Guys started pushing each other. I immediately jumped in to break it up. I was trying to protect Joe.

A few months earlier, Joe had had surgery on his shoulder.

"You wanna come out?" I asked him after the scrum.

"Hell, no!"

I knew Joe was pissed.

Next play, the offense ran a bubble screen. I looked back and Joe was swinging at Patrick Queen, one of our linebackers. Before I knew it, we had a full-scale brawl.

I think that set the tempo for us. He was saying: "Our offense ain't gonna take no more s***."

I said, "Joe, you can't be fighting. Come on, man." He nodded. Then, the offense went in the red zone and torched the defense. It was ugly for the defense. That was the day we completed 80 percent of our passes. They outschemed them. Guys were wide open. I told Derek Ponamsky right then after that practice, "We are going to have one hell of a football team."

You could see the confidence growing within the offense.

I wanted our guys to get into a froth. We called it "fire in the hole." We just didn't want anyone breaking a hand in a fight on the practice field. When it gets closer to the season, we eliminate all fighting. I make sure they know that we're not going to have any foolish penalties. With two weeks left in camp, they know there is no more fighting. Next guy who fights, the whole team has to run.

I was two months out of surgery. I shouldn't have really been taking reps, but I was taking reps. I got tackled by JaCoby. It kind of tweaked my shoulder and there was a little scuffle. I got up and realized that I wasn't in it. It was other people. So the next play, I was looking for something to get another one started, because I wasn't in the first one. Patrick was talking smack in my face, so I kinda started a brawl there. That was probably the biggest brawl we had. That was just a microcosm of the entire spring being super intense and competitive. We were kicking the defense's ass all spring. I don't know what they'll tell you about it—I don't know what the defense has said—but we were kicking their ass, and I think they got kind of tired of it. They hadn't been used to that.

—*JOE BURROW*

I have coached a lot of tough guys and been around some excellent quarterbacks. But I had never seen a quarterback in the middle of those fights, and certainly not like Joe was.

It was the most unbelievable thing I've ever seen. After practice, Joe's face was all scratched up. I was dang fired up. For years, our offense didn't have an identity. Joe had that hard edge. He gave us an identity on offense, and everybody bought in. Then, it just took off.

—*TOMMY MOFFITT, LSU HEAD STRENGTH COACH*

We had started to focus on the little details that always make the big things work well. We were coming together as a team and we were ready.

◄17

THE NEW LSU

Later in spring 2019, our athletic director changed at LSU. Joe Alleva was forced out. Scott Woodward was hired from Texas A&M to replace him. Right away, you could feel the impact Scott was making. From the get-go, he brought a championship mindset.

Scott had graduated from LSU. He worked as the school's director of external affairs in the early 2000s when LSU won a national title. He knew what was important to have success at LSU. Football was given a green light: whatever we needed to compete at a championship level, he was all for. We added more analysts to our staff. We could feel the commitment from him, and the players really liked him. I think because we are both from Louisiana, we both understood the power of LSU football.

Before training camp started, our trainer, Jack Marucci, came to speak to me. Jack was kind of like my guru. He was not your typical trainer. He is, by far, the best I have ever been around. He did amazing analytical studies and projects. His mind stretches way outside the box. I gave him the freedom to explore the mental and physical aspects of our team. I always listened to what he had to say. I really think Jack is a genius—but a mild-mannered genius. He's so unassuming that he does everything in the background and doesn't want credit for it.

Jack told me that our 2019 team had the highest character he'd ever graded in his two decades at LSU. He said that was a good indicator that we were fixing to have a special season. It lined up with my feeling about the group we had coming back, but Jack had come up with a way to quantify it, and it made a lot of sense.

Evaluating these guys from that recruiting class (2017), they were going to be our leaders. I knew we were gonna have a heck of a year based off of those numbers. I think that's one reason we were able to sustain the level we did. I talk to scouts about this all the time. They want to know how that team was built and how we were able to keep this level. Obviously, we had good players, but we've had good players before. What's the difference with those good players? It's got to be something.

The biggest piece was character. Character guys are the ones who, when things don't go quite right, they're not going to complain as much. They're not going to sink the ship. They're not going to point fingers. They can rally the troops better—because you're going to have adversity. It's inevitable. Sometimes, you get seduced by the talent and say, "I gotta have that guy," but does that guy have enough character? I always knew it in my gut, but I had nothing to prove it. There was something to being around those type of people and the success they had. We won a national championship when I was at Florida State [1993]. I started looking at that team. It was Charlie Ward. It was Derrick Brooks. It was Warrick Dunn. Yes, great talent but extremely high-character guys. When LSU won in '03, we had Matt Mauck, Ben Wilkerson, and some of these players. We won in '07 with Matt Flynn, Craig Steltz, and that group. How was I going to quantify this stuff?

There are really four traits we look for: two subjective and two objective. The most important one is subjective. We look at academics—are they on the lists we get every day? We look at drug use—we test a lot—and if they have any off-the-field issues. We look at coachability: Are they very defiant? It's easy to see it. Do they take coaching? I watched one of our players get ripped because we had him on the sideline looking at him in the tent, and he ran out on the field and missed a call. It was our fault probably. His position coach lit into him and he didn't even flinch. Some players would have been defiant. The most important [character area] to me is, how do they treat people in the building? I will ask our student trainers, "Give me your top ten, and give me your bottom ten. When you interact, do you have problems with them?" That to me reveals the best character. They probably don't think they have to show respect dealing with students or people in our training room area even. You check with the cafeteria people, all the auxiliary pieces, sports information. We get feedback from all of these groups, and it doesn't vary much.

Then, I looked at the highest character classes we've had: five of the top six had all played for or won a national championship. This class was loaded with so many good kids. That was Grant Delpit's class, Clyde, JaCoby Stevens, K'Lavon Chaisson, Jacob Phillips, Justin Jefferson, Todd Harris, Ed Ingram, Pat Queen, Racey McMath, Austin Deculus—Ed's first recruiting class here. So many good character guys. And then you add in Joe [Burrow], a grad transfer and fifth-year senior.

—*JACK MARUCCI, LSU DIRECTOR OF ATHLETIC TRAINING*

Joe Burrow was a two-hundred-to-one Heisman long shot before the season. I knew he was going to have a great year, but I never imagined the level of productivity we would reach.

During training camp, I brought Joe into my office. I said, "You make sure that you're running the plays that you feel like you can be the most successful at, and you let me know if you need anything." I knew he loved that we were going to more empty—with no running backs in the backfield—because it made the defense declare what it was going to do. He liked the quarterback runs, the deep balls, the use of our tight ends; he really liked the control of changing protections on the line of scrimmage. Some of that, he was used to doing before. I just wanted to make sure he knew that he had the green light to go to Steve and Coach Joe and tell them what he wanted. And that gave Joe ownership. I had never told another quarterback anything like that.

Joe knew his guys. The way he studied football, he was like a player-coach. He knew talent. He knew his guys' personalities. He knew what they did well and what they didn't do well. Most guys in college are just focusing on doing their own job. He knew what everybody else was supposed to be doing.

We had a mature team, led by Joe. They only gave us very minor problems. Joe wouldn't put up with it. If guys were screwing around, he would call them out in a heartbeat. They listened to him; they had respect for a guy who was playing at his level and had displayed the kind of toughness and character that he had.

I'd ask him, "What time do you think curfew ought to be? What do y'all want to eat?" And he'd get in on the details. As we got into the season, I gave him even more ownership of the team. Joe was probably the most critical person in the building. I could be the good cop, and I didn't have to be critical of the team, especially on offense.

> Coach O and the staff put a lot of trust in the players to figure it out on our own. A big reason that we were so good [in 2019] is because Coach O, Coach Joe, and Coach E all knew that I knew what I was talking about, so they trusted my input, and trusted that if I had a concept that I wanted to put in, they put it in the next day. If it worked, it stayed in; and if it didn't work, they took it out. When your coaches have that much trust in you, it's easy on the field because you don't have to think about it. If you want to do something, you just do it.

> —JOE BURROW

We played Georgia Southern in our 2019 season opener. They had won ten games in 2018. We weren't about to take anyone lightly. Joe tied a school record with five touchdown passes. We completed passes to fourteen different receivers. Our defense held them under one hundred total yards. We won, 55–3.

Week two, we had to play number nine Texas on the road.

I figured the media would probably play up the angle of me facing Tom Herman's team, but I wasn't going to get into any of that. I had no concern about blocking out that chatter. The real challenge was their quarterback, Sam Ehlinger. He reminded me of Tim Tebow, but was a better passer. We knew we were going to have our hands full with him.

I didn't expect the environment in that game. I had always heard that even for a pretty big stadium, Texas had a quiet crowd. That was not my experience. The place was rocking. That game was like a Super Bowl to them, like we were in a big heavyweight fight. It felt like a big SEC game.

We got into a wild back-and-forth game with Texas. Joe was on fire. Ehlinger got hot in the second half. The Longhorns scored to cut our lead down to 37–31 with 3:59 left in the game. Before our offense came back onto the field, I said to Steve over the headset, "Hey, what do you think about going four-minute offense?"

"No. We're going to pass the ball. Go down there and score again."

I said, "Okay, go ahead!"

We moved the ball close to midfield. Joe threw on first down. Incomplete. He had completed thirteen passes in a row before that. Second down. They blitzed him off the corner. Sacked. It was third-and-seventeen from our thirty-nine-yard line with 2:34 left. Texas called timeout.

I think most people were expecting us to play it safe and call a run play to get them to burn their last timeout. Steve called four verticals. I looked at Mickey Joseph, our receivers coach, and said, "If this doesn't work, they're going to kill me in Baton Rouge."

They blitzed again. All-out blitz. Clyde stepped up and blocked the linebacker coming up the middle. He got him just enough to allow Joe to slide to his left and buy Justin Jefferson a little more time to get open. Joe hit Justin right in stride on a crossing route, and he took off down the sideline. Touchdown, LSU.

That was one of the most defining plays of our season, and of my career. Joe stepped up and made a miraculous play. Any other quarterback would have gotten sacked if they didn't have the pocket presence and awareness he had to get free for just a split-second longer to buy his guy a little more time.

I trusted our guys, and it was beautiful. Seeing Justin running into the end zone, I said to myself, "We've got a team. We've got some playmakers." I believed we had a real shot to win the national title. Texas gave us their best shot, and we beat them. It was the first time in LSU history we ever had three receivers go over one hundred yards in a game. After the game, Joe Burrow said we still had room for improvement—that we were going to get better.

He was right.

We blew past Northwestern State, Vandy, and Utah State to get to 5–0 before number seven Florida visited Tiger Stadium. The Gators were a big challenge. It's a heated rivalry. You may not realize it outside of LSU or Florida. I didn't realize it was such a nasty rivalry till I got to LSU. For some reason, our team doesn't like them and they don't like us.

Before when we played them, I knew we had to stop the fighting. The players were almost more concerned with fighting them than beating them. Whenever they had beaten us, we'd had too many turnovers and too many penalties. We settled that down. I told the team before the game, "We don't like Florida. I get it. But let's beat them when the ball is snapped."

Dan Mullen's teams have given us a hard time. They're always the best-coached teams we play. They gave us some problems, flexing out their tight end. But they couldn't stop Clyde. Then Joe heated up in the second half and went 21 of 24 and had as many touchdown passes as he did incompletions. We won, 42–28. We really needed the crowd, and the fans came through. They helped win the game for us.

We came into the game against number nine Auburn averaging over fifty points per game. Auburn did something it had never done before defensively. They played this funky 3–1–7 look to try and throw us off. It worked for a little while, but Clyde was eating them up. He ran for over 130 yards. We still had thirty first downs and more than 500 yards. We won, 23–20.

We were 8–0 going into a bye week, headed to Alabama. We were ranked number two. They were ranked number three. I'm sure a lot of people only thought about Alabama's winning streak over LSU going into that game in Tuscaloosa. But they weren't seeing what I saw every day.

◄

Our team had a perfect balance. Our guys were locked in, but they were also very loose and loaded with confidence, in themselves and in each other. Jack's character evaluation of this team was so accurate. We had way fewer guys than normal appearing on lists for discipline issues; very few guys missed classes, treatments, or team meals. Almost everybody was early for everything. That had become their standard, and there was a direct correlation over to the football field.

The best part was seeing how many guys had matured in their time with us. Thaddeus Moss, the son of the great Randy Moss, didn't play in 2018 because of injuries and was rarely able to practice.

We just never knew what we had in him. I think his friendship with Joe Burrow made a difference with Thaddeus. When the culture of the team says that character is cool, it counts. That wakes people up. I think Thaddeus was tired of being seen as an underachiever. In the off-season, he didn't go home for spring break. He got in shape. He cut his hair. He became a factor. He started realizing his potential, and his confidence grew.

Tyler Shelvin, our huge nose tackle who always battled weight issues, made a ton of progress in his work ethic. He kept his weight down and became a dominant force for us. I think he noticed Rashard Lawrence's work ethic in practice and how he gave everything he had for LSU. That made a difference on our football team.

Adrian Magee, who'd been a freshman scout team offensive lineman when I first got to LSU, grew up a lot. He had been overweight. He wasn't serious about football. He wasn't serious about anything. He was kind of a jokester—not a bad kid, but not necessarily one to be counted on. Adrian is very close to his mother, and I think she kept on pushing and motivating him to graduate and do well. I give his mama, Miss Nicki, and James Cregg a lot of credit. Coach Cregg saw there was something special there, and Adrian turned into a very good lineman for us.

JaCoby Stevens had become a team leader for us. He had come in as a five-star recruit and didn't get settled into a spot for a little while, but that year he took more of a vocal leadership role, and that made a big difference. He's a great practice player, and he would challenge his teammates, "Hey man, we gotta practice better!"

Patrick Queen was another guy whose development epitomized the spirit of our program. When Devin White left for the NFL after the 2018 season, we moved Michael Divinity inside to linebacker, so we had Patrick, Jacob Phillips, and Divinity competing for those two jobs. Midway through training camp, Patrick and his parents asked to have a meeting with me. They thought he wasn't going to start, and they were a little upset. Obviously, in this day of the transfer portal, I was thinking he wanted to leave. Instead, Patrick came to me and said, "What do I need to do to get better?" His dad, who had played football at Nicholls State, said, "Just tell the boy what he needs to get better at."

I said we wanted to see Patrick become more physical at the point of attack, come to practice with more energy, and be more vocal. Patrick was always a quiet guy, but after that meeting, he turned into one of the best linebackers in the country, flying around the field and making plays sideline-to-sideline. He ended up as a first-round pick.

Younger guys like Cordale Flott and Jay Ward, two true freshman cornerbacks, made our practices better because they went so hard. Our second-team offensive line was flying us around giving us a damn good look every day. The guys really bought into that system.

Young guys were blossoming before our eyes. Our receivers had been busting their tails from the moment the last season ended. They'd worked hard to get their timing down with Joe. They had such a bond with Mickey Joseph, their position coach, and when Joe Brady arrived they immediately bought in and embraced what he was preaching.

We watched how Justin Jefferson kept developing from a two-star recruit who his teammates thought was a walk-on to a first-round talent, because he gave everything he had in practice. We saw how Ja'Marr Chase broke out and became the best receiver in college football because he was so physical and fast and honed his chemistry with Joe Burrow. I loved watching Ja'Marr and our great freshman cornerback Derek Stingley Jr. go at it in one-on-ones every day. They were two of the best players in the country at their respective positions—a prime example of iron sharpening iron. It was beautiful to watch. Our third receiver, Terrace Marshall, had healed from a broken right leg he had suffered before he came to LSU; he became a playmaker too. Those guys knew that Coach Joe and Steve would get them open, and Joe Burrow would get them the ball.

Players were developing, and our practices reached another level, similar to what I'd encountered at USC under Pete Carroll or at Miami under Jimmy Johnson. By 2019 we had achieved that level at practice at LSU.

The way we executed, you could just feel the crispness and the attention to detail. The guys knew their roles. You could tell they took pride in what they were doing; they took pride in who they had become. Our simulation was better than it had ever been; practices were cleaner, sharper. There weren't a lot of busts. The guys behind them were clapping, providing more energy, going hard. We didn't need to pump in music at practice to try and get guys fired up. We had our own juice and brought the energy ourselves. If you don't have a very special team, football practices are often not like that. With this 2019 group, it didn't seem like practice was a chore. It caught fire.

Pete Carroll used to say to me, "Go back to your practices. That'll tell you how your team is going to play in the game." And if we didn't win a game, I would go back and watch practice. Sure enough, I could tell. I learned a lot of lessons from those losses. I can still hear his voice: "Watch it, Eddie! Everybody wants to just jump on to the next opponent, but you gotta figure why you lost first."

When we lost to Florida in 2018, we had fumbles, dropped balls, and missed assignments, and we didn't execute properly on defense. They ran for over two hundred yards on us and did a lot of damage with the speed option. I went back and watched our practice film from the previous week. I saw that we didn't rep it enough, and when we did rep it, we didn't play it right in practice. Our outside linebacker needed to slow-play it on the line of scrimmage.

Instead, we attacked it in practice. Our linebacker had the pitch man and he was fast-playing and getting blocked by their tackle. I saw our mistake on the practice film.

I'm a stickler for simulation. In order for our guys to play things correctly, we have to show them many times in practice and rep it right. When it comes to practice, it's details, details, details. That stuff is my expertise. I'm going to give them the very best of what I know. That's what I've done for thirty-five years, and I get to set the tempo and the tone.

In 2018, we beat Georgia by twenty points, but I knew they gashed us pretty good in the running game with their inside zone, or at least they did early before we adjusted. Well, even after that big win, I took something from it. We started doing our "bump combo" drill every Tuesday at practice. We practiced the heck out of it, and it added physicality and toughness to our team—because that drill *is* the SEC. It's a bump-combo league. That's at the heart of what makes the SEC so physical. If you can't handle it, you can't win in this league. So I knew we needed to ramp up that physicality, as well as the precision that needs to go with it, into our routine.

We would line up a guard and a tackle and have them go against a shaded three-technique (defensive tackle) and a linebacker. Those O-linemen have to double-team the three technique, but then the guard has to come off and block the linebacker. As soon as the guard comes off, the running back hits the hole as hard as he can. That makes it very difficult for the defensive lineman. We run that drill using a center and guard; a guard and tackle; a tackle and tight end. Everybody's into it.

In the SEC especially, that bump combo comes into play on the inside zone, the outside zone, and power plays. You've got to play that block, and the defensive players have to work together. They've got to get their footwork and pad level down. The offensive lineman has to block a linebacker on the second level, which is not easy for them, because in our league, you've got first-rounders all over the place. It teaches the back just where to hit the crease. It's a very disciplined, tough-ass drill. It's a way of going full speed but not taking guys to the ground. I think it's better than going eleven-on-eleven or scrimmaging because it still gives you that physicality. And, they have to be ready for physicality in the SEC on Saturdays.

Midway through the season, I backed off on the bump combo. The players started smiling, because they knew it took a lot of energy and they appreciated me trying to take care of their bodies. You have got to know your team.

We made another change that paid off that year—something I think is very rare in college football. We only had one full-staff meeting a week. I realized that I had a staff I really trusted. Those guys were in working at 6:00 a.m. Before, I felt like we were just having a staff meeting to have a staff meeting. In the past, I heard how those meetings might start a half hour late and drag on for ninety minutes. That just sucked the energy out of the football building. Now we meet just one time during the week. We have support staff, academics, and recruiting in there. We cover schedules and whatever we need to cover. We give them the plan, and we're going to roll.

Our communication is so good on my current staff that I don't have to go over these things. We trust each other. I trust our coordinators. In 2019 we had Steve, Greg McMahon with special teams, and Dave Aranda. Just having that one weekly meeting is one of the best things we have ever done. You don't have to stop your offensive or defensive meetings or your film breakdown. That's a half hour where you don't have to interrupt your work. I know our staff appreciated it. We're not hounding them. We're showing we trust them and letting them do their jobs.

This was the new LSU—and we were banking on trust.

◀18

I I I I I I I I I I I

GETTING TO 9-0
IN TUSCALOOSA

By the Monday of Alabama week, I knew we were going to beat them. I didn't think they could stop our offense. I felt it would be a high-scoring game, but I didn't think they had the same caliber of defensive line they'd had in the past. And they didn't. We finally had the right scheme for them. Our guys weren't intimidated by them at all.

I told the team that Monday, "Guys, we are the better team. Now, we've got to practice like it, and prepare like it. Then we've got to play like it. And, I know we will."

We went ninety-two yards on our first six plays to take a 7–0 lead. They fumbled on their first series. Then, on their next series, we forced them to punt and their punter fumbled the snap. We took a 10–0 lead and kept attacking. Joe Burrow completed his first thirteen passes of the game. Alabama got us on a long punt return, where their kid made an amazing play. We had a 19–13 lead late in the second quarter. Joe started leading us down the field. He picked up eleven yards on a quarterback draw. Next play, he scrambled for nineteen more. One play later, he connected with Justin Jefferson—another first down. Next play, Joe threw a strike, back-shoulder to Thaddeus, who pulled it in with his body falling out of bounds, but he was able to keep his toes in bounds to set us up at the one-yard line.

Alabama's crowd sounded pretty sure the refs were going to overturn the play. The Jumbotron showed that Thaddeus's foot was out of bounds before he caught the ball, but he was able to get his foot back in, then catch the ball and get his feet down in bounds.

The rule was, if a receiver is forced out of bounds due to contact by a defender, the receiver can reestablish position on the field and make a legal catch. They ruled on the field that Thaddeus had been forced out of bounds by contact. And, by rule, if there was contact between the defender and the receiver, whether or not the receiver was forced out of bounds is not reviewable. I was thinking, *You know what? Tonight's our night.* It was very rare that you go play at Alabama and get those calls. Everything was going our way.

As they were reviewing the play, the official said to me, "Hey, that should be a catch." It felt like that replay review took about four minutes.

Watching Thaddeus's catch along the sideline against Alabama with the officials reviewing it like that—whether he'd been forced out of bounds or not by the Bama defensive back—it hit me, *There was something about the play. Man, have I been through this before?*

I didn't make the connection till a little later to that play the refs overturned when I was coaching at Ole Miss and Shay Hodge made that catch along the Alabama sideline during the final minute in my very first game coaching against Nick Saban and my last season with Ole Miss. It was pretty eerie.

When I thought back to that moment from that Alabama-Ole Miss game and how it didn't make sense how they could've overturned that catch at such a critical moment like that, and then to see Thaddeus's catch along the sidelines against this Crimson Tide team and for it to go in our favor, I thought, *There is a God above. It came back to us.*

We got first-and-goal at the Alabama one-yard line. Clyde ran it in, and we went up 26–13. Everything was going our way.

Alabama got the ball back with twenty-six seconds left in the half. Patrick Queen intercepted Tua Tagovailoa on the next play. We had the ball inside the red zone with eleven seconds left. Joe connected with Clyde for a touchdown pass. We went up 33–13 at halftime.

We got back to our locker room. I was worried about us relaxing and letting down our guard. I knew nothing was going to be easy. Defeating Alabama was going to take sixty minutes. I challenged them, "Can we keep this standard up for thirty minutes more?"

"Guys, it's 0–0," I told them. "We have come too far, guys. We're playing Alabama. Let's go! Let's go out-physical them. Don't even look at the scoreboard."

In the second half, Alabama did rally, but we kept making plays. Joe kept torching their defense. Clyde was making their guys miss. Running over their guys. Dragging their guys. The determination he played with in a game of that magnitude—holy smokes!—was as dominant a performance by any running back as I have ever seen. Clyde went for 180 rushing and receiving yards, and most of those yards came after contact. He ran for three touchdowns and caught a fourth.

Clyde always had confidence in himself. He had come in as a three-star recruit and played with a chip on his shoulder. He didn't talk about it, though. He played that way.

Joe went 31 of 39 for 393 yards and ran for 96 more yards. We won 46–41, scoring the most points anyone had against an Alabama defense since Nick Saban had been there.

After the game, we were emotional. It had been a long eight years for the state of Louisiana not being able to beat Alabama. A few things I told the team in the locker room got out after one of our players posted what he'd recorded on his cell phone onto social media.

Things are going to be said in the locker room after a big win like that. I talked to the team about it, about keeping our private moments in the locker room private. Keep them in the family. I certainly didn't want that to get out like that. I respect Nick Saban and their program. I'd never try to disrespect that man, especially after all he has done for college football.

When the player who had filmed it came to me, he had his head down. He was nervous. I said, "You made a mistake. Let's just make sure we don't do that again, okay?" And that was that. It was over as far as I was concerned. It was what I would have told my own kid after making a mistake.

When I was at Ole Miss, if something like that would have happened, I would have overreacted. I probably would have berated the kid. Punished him. Then that probably would have gotten into the media, and then, it would have become an even bigger deal. That's how a twenty-four-hour story becomes a seventy-two-hour story—making it into a bigger problem.

When my wife and I pulled onto our street at around 11:00 that night after beating Alabama, about thirty neighborhood kids were in our driveway, from about ages six to twelve. They were standing with their parents. They had made signs and posted them up all over our house. It was amazing to see the joy on their faces. They had made a big banner and had me run through it, like I was back on the high school team before a big game. Their reaction was one of the most gratifying moments I've ever had as a coach. It was a treat to celebrate that moment with them.

◀

We went to Ole Miss the next week as the new number one team in the country. We beat the Rebels, 58–37. The winner of that rivalry game of the "Magnolia Bowl" gets the Magnolia Trophy. Nobody on our team picked it up. We didn't even really think about it. I discussed it with Joe Burrow; we were going to leave it up to him.

Nope, we weren't celebrating the Magnolia Trophy. That was Joe and the team's mindset. Nobody was going to be satisfied with that. We had bigger goals.

We followed that up by beating Arkansas, 56–20, and Texas

A&M, 50–7. That was our seniors' last home game. It was a statement game—especially since the year before we couldn't stop them on defense. Our guys had a chip on their shoulders. There was electricity in the air. I knew there was no way they were going to come in and beat us. It was on. The defense really stood up.

We improved exponentially as the season went on. We caught fire. We tightened up on defense. Our guys loved to practice, and our practices were so good. I very seldom had to say anything to them about crispness or good energy.

There was plenty of chatter about our season outside the building, but I kept reminding them to block out the noise. Every week, we had to reel them back. Sometimes when you're losing, your guys can go in the tank. But when you keep winning, especially the way we were winning and how we were the hot new thing in football, my job is to get them back to even keel every week. Joe Burrow helped a lot on that front. He'd get on the offense if he saw any sign of slippage. If they left any points out there, he always told the truth. I loved that about him.

When we won the SEC West title after we beat A&M, we didn't want any hats commemorating the division title. We didn't want any T-shirts. We didn't have any celebration.

That was not our final destination.

I never mentioned the words *national championship* to the team. I learned that from Pete Carroll. We only talked about skill development and continuing to get better. The players caught wind of it, and they didn't talk about it either. They just wanted to follow the program.

◀

We had number four Georgia up next in the SEC title game in Atlanta. Some of our staff had heard about how the Bulldogs wanted to get revenge for us beating them by twenty points a year earlier in Baton Rouge, and that they were looking to do to us what we'd just done to the Aggies.

We were a different team, though.

On our opening series of the SEC Championship, we went seventy-five yards on eight plays to score a touchdown. They were defending us a bit like Auburn tried to. Georgia hadn't shown a single snap of that defense all season, but Joe Burrow still picked it apart, starting the game 10 of 12 with two touchdown passes. We jumped out to a 14–0 lead, and before the third quarter was over, it was 34–3. Much of the dome, which was mostly Georgia red, had emptied out. We scored twice as many points as the Bulldogs had given up in any game all year. We sacked their quarterback three times and shut down their running game. Our guys were happy in the locker room, but they weren't going crazy. We knew we had two more games to win.

Before the College Football Playoff, we had to go on the awards circuit, which we juggled with recruiting and the early signing period. We went to Atlanta for the college football awards show. They should have held it in Baton Rouge, because it was like the LSU show in there. I think we took home six awards. It was such a proud week for our program.

We got to New York at the end of the week, where Joe Burrow was the overwhelming favorite to win the Heisman. He deserved it for all he had done for our program at LSU. That was the first time I'd ever been at the Heisman. It's a who's who of the greats of the game. Mike Garrett was there, Billy Sims, Marcus Allen, Doug Flutie, lots of guys I grew up watching. We were surrounded by greatness.

Joe won by the largest margin of victory in Heisman history. I was so proud seeing him accept, and proud that he showed how much he cared about the people of Southeast Ohio and where he came from that he ended up raising a half-million dollars for people in need there. During his speech, he completely surprised me when he started talking about me and what I meant to him. I wasn't expecting all that. Joe got very emotional. He got choked up. And so did I. He's not a man of many words, so it was an honor to hear him speak about how much he valued our relationship in front of the whole country.

> I had three or four bullet points on a piece of paper. But other than that, I was just saying what I felt and spoke from the heart. I really do feel that way about Coach O. He saved my career and made me what I am today and gave me the opportunity to prove myself, and for that, I'm forever grateful.
>
> —*JOE BURROW*

Joe took a chance on us, and we took a chance on him. It truly was a leap of faith by both of us.

> The biggest thing for me was to see that he had felt so deeply about his relationships there at LSU. When he was at Ohio State, he developed some great friendships with his teammates and had built some strong trust with a few graduate assistants, but otherwise, it was a business relationship with the coaches there. In that short amount of time he was in Baton Rouge, we saw how he came to love and appreciate his coaches and teammates at LSU. That made me very happy. He ended up with a special bond with Coach O that stems from a mutual appreciation of each other. Joe was able to trust everything that Coach O said.
>
> —*ROBIN BURROW, JOE'S MOM*

◀19

WINNING EVERYTHING

The week before the playoff semifinal game against Oklahoma, Clyde Edwards-Helaire, our star running back, tweaked his hamstring at the end of a practice. We treated it, and he made a lot of progress leading up to the game. The night before the game, Clyde tested his hamstring out vigorously for the first time since hurting it. Clyde was cutting and accelerating, and he looked really good on the field. We had to see how it felt the next day, though. We were optimistic, but we also felt comfortable with the guys behind him. Chris Curry had been running hard in practice, and he had really stepped up. Joe Burrow had come to us and pushed for Chris to become the starter if Clyde couldn't be the main guy against Oklahoma. Chris wasn't as hyped a recruit as our two freshman running backs Tyrion Davis-Price and John Emery were, but that didn't matter. I told the guys, "Y'all just play the best guy."

Clyde had bounced back pretty well, but we had him on a pitch count to about fifteen plays. Chris Curry did exactly as we expected him to. He ran hard and had eighty-nine yards on sixteen carries. Our passing game had another big night. The Sooners' defense hadn't allowed a three-hundred-yard passing game all season, but Joe put up over four hundred on them in the first half. We won, 63–28. Justin Jefferson had a playoff-record fourteen catches for 227 yards and four touchdowns. Our defense, which had gotten healthier since the middle of the season, was playing faster and did a good job against a dangerous offense. We had won our two games at the dome in Atlanta against the number four and number five teams in the country, by a combined score of 110–38. We had beaten Georgia handily, and then came back to the same building and hung

63 on somebody in the College Football Playoff semifinal—wow! Our team was getting better and better as the season went on. We were so confident, so loose and focused. We really were on a mission. You could feel it. I knew we weren't going to take Clemson for granted, but I also didn't think anybody could beat us.

◀

Preparation for the national title game was key for us. I heard that other schools would do nine days of straight practice in between the semifinal and the title game. We treated it just like a bowl game. We practiced Monday through Thursday morning, and then I gave them time off until Monday—and then we had a regular game week. We didn't go nine days or eight days plus one. They had almost a full four days off.

Many other coaches asked me after the game, "How'd your guys look so fresh?" The answer is how we prepared. Our guys know I'm going to take care of them. Now, I am going to demand great practices and great execution, but I'm also not going to go too long and beat them up. And they love that. It's a part of their success.

The day before the title game, we had a brief staff meeting at noon. I started by telling the guys about a TV interview I had with ESPN earlier in the morning, with Clemson coach Dabo Swinney.

ESPN asked both of us if we had a question for the other coach. Dabo said to me, "Would you sit Joe Burrow for a quarter?"

I let Dabo's question hang in the air for about ten seconds before I told the staff in our meeting, "I almost said, 'I'm planning on lettin' him sit out that fourth quarter.'" All the guys starting laughing.

I had sensed that our staff was a little tight that weekend leading up to the game. I wanted to loosen them up. Now, I think the old Ed Orgeron would have actually said that line about sitting Joe in front of the cameras. Instead, I think my answer to Dabo's question was, "How do you tackle [Clemson running back] Travis Etienne?" I didn't want to say anything disrespectful to Dabo Swinney. He is a class act, and one of the best coaches in football. Before the game, after the game, he is the same person.

I told my staff that story because I remember how Pete Carroll would instill confidence in us, his staff, before a big game at USC. Pete said, "Hey guys, relax. We're going to win tomorrow." As an assistant, hearing him talk like that made me feel better. And Pete was often right.

◀

We practiced that afternoon the day before the game at the Saints facility. Drew Brees spoke to our team. I always wanted to surround our team with greatness, whether it was Marcus Allen, a Hall of Fame coach like John Robinson, or Drew Brees. The Saints had been very supportive of LSU. It was like we were brothers. If I could bring elite guys around our team, it was only going to help them. That day at practice, Drew was there with his three young sons. One had a Joe Burrow jersey on. Another one of his boys had on Clyde's jersey, and the third one had on Ja'Marr Chase's. What a feeling that must have been for our players, seeing that.

My speech to the team in our hotel the night before the title game lasted about fifteen minutes. I wanted them to know that I had all the confidence in the world in them. They had bought into the LSU standard of performance, and bought into it more than any championship team I've ever been around. I wanted to honor them because they had embraced what separated good from great, and that all started with character.

"You were early for curfews. Early for meetings. Relentless work ethic. You've kept this hotel clean. I've asked you to do it, and you did. No bulls***. Character. Character wins.

"Poise. No matter what happens, we go to the next play. Poise on the sideline. Poise on the headsets. Poise at halftime. Discipline. You just don't wake up and say, 'I'm going to be disciplined.' That don't happen! You're early. You work your ass off. You don't go do the things that you're not supposed to do. We set the LSU standard of performance, and up to now, nobody has come close to you when you're playing up to the LSU standard of performance.

"Your best will be good enough, and you will play your best tomorrow night. Why wouldn't you? You've done it fourteen times in a row. I think we're going to play our best game tomorrow night."

I emphasized how important ball security was, how LSU was 24–2 when it won the turnover battle, how it had beaten six top-ten teams in the country already, and to not give any of their energy to the TV tomorrow. One of the last things I talked about was Joe Burrow.

"Other teams' quarterbacks get hit and they b****," I said. "Our quarterback gets hit and I'm happy because I know he's pissed off, and he's bringing hell with him. That's the mindset."

When we went to bed that night, we were primed to have the best day of our lives.

◀

I knew Clemson was a really good football team. They had won twenty-nine in a row. We would have to play well on defense. When the game started, though, we weren't playing very well on defense. Then we got pinned deep in our own territory. We weren't moving the ball. But I always felt that we were going to come back.

Clemson's defense was, by far, the most aggressive group we had seen on film. They blitzed more than 60 percent of the time. We had to punt on our first three possessions. Their defensive coordinator, Brent Venables, is really good, but you can't zero-blitz us all the time. If you do, you're going to end up with Ja'Marr Chase in one-on-one situations, and that was a tough business proposition for any defensive back.

They had burned us with a couple of big plays, and by the second quarter, we were down 17–7—our biggest deficit of the season. That was the only time I got a little nervous, but Joe hit a couple more big plays to Ja'Marr and we got to 17–14. We started making adjustments. We stopped them on the next couple of series. Joe got comfortable. Ja'Marr took over. He was just too strong for them. He's got speed, but he also has so much strength—strong hands and a strong lower body. He was great at beating press coverage. They couldn't handle him.

Our defense played outstanding for a big stretch in the second and third quarters. Patrick Queen made some great plays on defense. We corralled Travis Etienne better than anybody else had all year. Our defense held them to one of eleven on third downs. Their quarterback, Trevor Lawrence, who looked great against Alabama in the title game the year before, didn't have a great night. We held him under 50 percent for the game.

Joe threw for 463 yards and five touchdowns. Ja'Marr had nine catches and 221 yards. The night before, Steve and Joe Brady had challenged our offense to be great in the red zone, and we were, scoring four touchdowns on five trips inside the twenty-yard line against a defense that had been as good at stopping teams as anyone in the country.

We won, 42–25. Standing there on the podium in our home state, I was overjoyed for our team. This was their win. I was also overjoyed for the state of Louisiana. I'd always wanted to hold that trophy up. I knew that was the benchmark for all LSU coaches. I had seen Nick Saban hold up that trophy when he was at LSU. I saw Les Miles hold it up. And now it was me.

It felt pretty surreal. I was trying to take things low-key and absorb everything about this special moment. I had a sense of satisfaction knowing that we had recruited all those guys. This was our program, and our family. I felt so fulfilled. It was the happiest day of my life.

This was the fifth time I'd been part of a national championship team, but this was night-and-day from those other celebrations. When you're an assistant, it feels terrific—but at the same time, those were Pete Carroll's teams. Those were Dennis Erickson's teams. This was my team. It felt amazing.

Was there a sense of vindication? Yeah, a little bit. But I didn't want to feel that way. I just didn't want to go there. I'd gotten over the hump. I wanted to be humble and give the credit to our team.

As wonderful as it was to celebrate with my family and my team, almost immediately afterward, the next day on the bus ride home, I started thinking about next year's team and how to win it all again. I was thinking, *Now I've got to replace all of these guys*. My mind immediately went to the future.

On the bus back to Baton Rouge, everybody was happy. Everybody was tired. The fans were screaming. Then I got a text.

Joe Brady's leaving.

I immediately went to talk to him on the bus. He told me the Carolina Panthers had shown interest in him before we left New Orleans. I was pretty sure he was leaving us. We would have to adjust once again, but I was grateful for everything he had done for us.

That ride home, though, was beyond enjoyable. So many of our fans had parked along the interstate to cheer. The best part of it for me was when we turned off the interstate and drove through the small towns. Cooks were coming out of restaurants. People were screaming and holding up signs. When we went by a construction site, the welders stopped what they were doing and cheered on the side of the road. I am getting choked up now just thinking about it.

Those are my people.

That is where I came from.

That is how I was raised.

That is Louisiana.

To see them so happy, to see them proud, that still hits me today. And the journey there has been a blessing, both the ups and the downs. Every time I had to rethink, adjust, and flip the script, God was bringing me closer to home and closer to victory.

> The way God brought him home to Louisiana. Honestly, this whole thing is nuts. I have always believed in God and been a Christian my whole life. My dad is a walking testimony. Seeing what God has done in my dad's life has made me believe even more—110 percent. I have seen it, firsthand. I think I got closer to God after seeing magic happen right in front of our face.
>
> —*CODY ORGERON*

That season—the win at Alabama, the SEC championship, beating Clemson in the Dome to win it all, standing on the podium with our team around me, that bus ride home, and sharing the title with the people of our state; each of those things—felt like a culmination of something that started long before 2019. And it won't end with it either.

To truly flip the script, you can't be afraid to fail. You must start that journey by first looking in the mirror, seeing what is there, and what isn't. Then, closing your eyes and visualizing what you hope to one day see, and then having the faith and commitment to allow it to happen. Because it can.

AFTERWORD

After having the greatest season in college football history, we knew we were going to lose some fantastic players to the NFL. We lost some terrific coaches, too, but I was excited after the way we started 2020 for this program to continue to play at the LSU standard of performance—and that standard was set by the 2019 team.

I loved our new staff in 2020. We landed a great recruiting class and had been very impressed with some of our early enrollees. We had a new defensive system with Bo Pelini coming in, replacing Dave Aranda who became the new head coach at Baylor. Everybody was fired up. We had a new quarterback, a new center. But we still had many players and coaches who knew what it took to accomplish what we did in 2019.

The first week of spring football we had a couple of terrific practices with excellent energy and focus. Myles Brennan, who was Joe's backup the previous two seasons, looked outstanding. So did Max Johnson and TJ Finley, our two freshman quarterbacks who had arrived on campus early. We were going to have our first day in pads. It was a Thursday in mid-March in 2020. I met with our athletic director Scott Woodward that day at noon.

"This thing is for real," Scott said. The COVID-19 pandemic had made its way to the United States and was about to hit Louisiana hard. "I don't know how much longer we're going to be practicing for."

We had a great practice that day. That night, we held our scheduled coaches clinic in Baton Rouge, with the most coaches we have ever had at LSU. We had scheduled a huge crawfish boil for them Friday night, but everything was changing fast. We had planned to have a big scrimmage on Saturday, but that was getting shut down. By Monday, our campus closed.

We realized we were dealing with something much bigger than football.

Our governor, John Bel Edwards, and I have become very close. He's been very supportive of me, and I have been very supportive of him. I think he does a great job. His office reached out to me that weekend to see if I would tape a PSA urging folks to take the necessary precautions. They wanted me to talk about "the game plan" of keeping people as safe as possible. We taped it that Saturday. I demonstrated how to properly cover your cough by coughing into your elbow. I talked about washing your hands thoroughly, for a full twenty seconds, and said, "If you are sick, stay home." I delivered the PSA much like I would if I was addressing my team.

I didn't know that PSA would go viral, but I am glad people saw it. The message was very important, and the more people we could reach, the better.

COVID-19 hit New Orleans hard. It became very real here, very fast. I was shocked at how quickly it hit home. Coaches on our staff lost family members. Our players lost grandparents, and some parents were hospitalized. We were alarmed. You don't really look at it quite like that until people in your family are affected.

The best thing I could do to help people, especially in the state of Louisiana, in the time of a pandemic was to use my voice and my platform as the head coach of the national champion LSU Tigers. It is a very powerful position in this state. I have always understood that. And responsibility comes with the job. My responsibility was to get the message out.

I know for the people here, the common man, the blue-collar person, they related to me. I am one of them. They get that. And I am honored to have that connection with them.

A week after the PSA, the governor invited me to sit in on a meeting he was leading, and later, to join him at a press conference. Some of the most important leaders in the state of Louisiana were in that meeting. I was so impressed by the governor. I saw real leadership from him in there. At the press conference, I delivered the game plan to the residents. It was a pep talk about staying home and being a good team member. The message we wanted people to take away was this: "It's going to get tough the next few weeks, but I believe in Louisiana. And, I believe we have a winning game plan."

Later, I appeared on ESPN and on Fox News, where the host asked what I'd tell people who didn't want to stay home.

"They need to take this seriously," I replied. "It could affect a lot of people's lives. I think that maturity needs to play a big part in what we're doing. We need to look at the overall picture, the overall health of our country and the people this may affect. They need to be accountable and stay home and follow the rules."

Within hours of being released, the PSA had over 2 million hits on our social media and had gone viral, making him the unofficial national spokesman. Even President Trump watched the PSA at a White House internal briefing after becoming a fan following his attendance at the 2019 College Football National Championship. Throughout our COVID-19 response, Coach O has been called upon by me and others with his recognizable voice and his "America's Coach" persona. There is no doubt that he assisted Louisiana and the nation in reducing the spread and potentially saving lives.

—*JOHN BEL EDWARDS, GOVERNOR OF LOUISIANA*

I am proud of the way LSU and the people of the great state of Louisiana stepped up to pitch in and take care of each other during the COVID-19 crisis. Together we are working to move as "one team, one heartbeat" to assist those in need. And I can't say this enough—*Geaux Tigers!*

ACKNOWLEDGMENTS

I want to give a special thanks to all of my former teammates, coaches, and teachers as well as to every player, coach, and staffer that I have been fortunate to have worked with. Thank you to the staff at HarperCollins Publishing, One Street Books, and Nelson Books for your work and ongoing support of *Flip the Script*.

ABOUT THE AUTHOR

Ed Orgeron is the head coach of the LSU Tigers football team, the college football champions.